A Garland Series

The English Stage
Attack and Defense 1577 - 1730

A collection of 90 important works
reprinted in photo-facsimile in 50 volumes

edited by
Arthur Freeman
Boston University

The Evil and Danger of Stage-Plays

by

Arthur Bedford

with a preface
for the Garland Edition by

Arthur Freeman

Garland Publishing, Inc., New York & London

1974

Library of Congress Cataloging in Publication Data

Bedford, Authur, 1668-1745.
  The evil and danger of stage-plays.

  Reprint of the 1706 ed. printed by W. Bonny, Bristol,
Eng. 1. Theater--Moral and religious aspects.
1. Title.
PN2047.B46 1974   792'.013   72-170479
ISBN 0-8240-0626-7

Preface

Arthur Bedford was born at Tiddenham or Tidenham, near Cheapstowe, Gloucestershire, some twenty-five miles from Bristol, in 1668, and went up to Brasenose College, Oxford, where he graduated B.A. in 1687/8 and proceeded M.A. in 1691. Ordained in 1688, he returned to his county and served as vicar of Temple-Church, Bristol, from 1692 to 1713. With the commotion initiated by Jeremy Collier's Short View *(1698) and its predictable replies, Bedford threw himself into the fray, at first with a relatively modest sermon preached 7 January 1705 at Temple-Church. Published as* Serious Reflections on the Scandalous Abuse and Effects of the Stage *by the congenial London printer William Bonny, now transplanted to Bristol and by 1703 "stark blind" (John Dunton), Bedford's sermon may have brought him to the attention of Wriothesley, Duke of Bedford, whose chaplain he became in the following year. It was occasioned, he says, by "the Acting of* Comedies *and* Tragedies *in* St. James's

Parish during the time of the Fair in the year 1704" and the actual building of "a Play-house *in the City of* Bath, *and the great Apprehensions that such a Design was carried on this city [Bristol]."* Inter alia, *the portent of a tempest which alarmed many in 1703 is evoked to warn citizens of Bristol of the course matters were taking. Bonny's advertisements comprise only attacks on the stage.*

But by 23 July 1705 a theatrical manager, Mr. Power, and his troupe had established a semi-permanent playhouse at Bristol, and had staged Love for Love *in defiance of Collier's extreme strictures and the antagonism alike of local authorities and clergy. One non-clerical opponent published a* Concio Laici *or* Layman's Sermon, *taking up cudgels where the Church had evidently left them (Bedford,* Evil and Danger, *pp. 12 ff.), but no copy of this attack has come to light. Conceivably it is the same "advertisement" cited as "lately shewn" in* Serious Reflections, *and printed to discourage further stage-playing. Subsequently there appeared* A Second Advertisement *concerning the Profaneness of the Play-House, of which only* B^8 *(16 pages, surely lacking the preliminaries) survives in the British Museum, and which is unreasonably attributed to Bedford by* BMC *and*

PREFACE

by Lowe. Its title implies a connection with the lost Concio Laici, *and its tone is more obviously secular than Bedford's; nor is it mentioned in the advertisements to* Evil and Danger *(1706) which do include* Serious Reflections *and a prior essay on the misuse of sacred music in popular domain. We do reprint the text of* A Second Advertisement, *but offer no claim for Bedford's authorship.*

The first of Bedford's two major assaults on the stage, The Evil and Danger of Stage-Plays, *appeared in the following year, once more printed by Bonny at Bristol, but now on sale, by Henry Mortlake, at London. A kind of sequel of Collier's* Short View *("Immorality and Profaneness": "Evil and Danger"), it claims to include "almost Two Thousand* Instances, *taken from the* Plays *of the two last Years, against all the* Methods *lately used for their* Reformation." *Treating briefly of the events at Bristol, account is given of Mr. Power's first playing of* Love for Love *(23 July 1705), as well as of* The Provok'd Wife *(13 August following), for which the company were sternly admonished and fined, and a temporary end to professional theatre in that city effected.*

Reverend Bedford obtained the living of Newton St. Loe, Somersetshire, in 1713, and probably remained there as rector some eleven years, although he did not resign the place until 1737. In 1719 he offered to the world a treatise on the literal immorality of the drama which is exceeded for scholastic and precisionist zeal not even by its spiritual forefather Histriomastix. A Serious Remonstrance in behalf of the Christian Religion . . . against . . . English Play-Houses *– now printed, as Lowe-Arnott-Robinson omit to mention, at London, by John Darby, for booksellers in Bath, Bristol, and Oxford – cites "almost Seven Thousand Instances [of profaneness and immorality] taken out of the Plays of the present Century, and especially of the five last Years," along with "above Fourteen Hundred Texts of Scripture, which are mentioned in this Treatise, either as ridicul'd and expos'd by the Stage, or as opposite to their present Practices," the latter catalogued in sixteen double-columned pages. Virtually unique of its kind, this exhaustive compendium speaks a long and desperately thorough immersion in the tainted literature (although as usual there is no indication of actual theater-going), and may stand as a high-water mark of pietistic/diabolist anti-theatrical paranoia. In* Evil and Danger *we learned that "God" is pronounced*

PREFACE

23 times in The Duchess of Malfi; *here we are confronted with the "wickedness" of even mocksorcery, the "blasphemy" of Macbeth, and the unforgivable attribution to human agency of such heavenly action or forbearance as love, luck, and safety. The extent of Bedford's imagination in identifying transgression is astounding: "When correctly viewed," as Mr. Lehrer puts it, latterly,* "everything *is lewd."*

In 1724 Bedford came to live at Hoxam, and subsequently held the post of Lecturer of St. Botolph's, Aldersgate. In this capacity he preached a sermon on 29 November 1729, "occasioned by the erecting of a play-house in the neighborhood," printed (1730) by Charles Akers for J. Hooke, W. Meadows, and T. Cox. "The Erecting of a Play-House *in the Neighbourhood obliges me to warn this Congregation of the great Evil and Danger in Frequenting them," he explains, but full twenty-five years after his similar preachment at Bristol, Bedford was not above putting his rhetoric to second use. With a few minimal rephrasings and omissions of local or timebound allusions, and a few updatings (notably a longish attack, pp. 22-5, on* The Beggar's Opera*) the new sermon is the old sermon* verbatim. *In an appendix Bedford cites as*

9

"unanswered" his larger works of 1706 and 1719. A "second edition" (for John Wilford, the pamphlet specialist, 1735; not in Lowe-Arnott-Robinson, British Museum 1112.e.18[1]) is no more than the 1730 sheets with a cancel title.

*The lucrative new playhouse in Goodman's Fields, opened by Thomas Odell 31 October 1729, was ordered closed on 28 April 1730 "because of the complaints of the Lord Mayor and Aldermen" (Nicholl, II, 284), but "under circumstances which are not clear, Odell commenced production again on 11 May and continued playing until the end of the regular season" (*London Stage, *III, xxii; cf. MLN, XXV [1930], 443-56). Garrick made his first London appearance here in 1741, and the playhouse was still in operation in 1742. It was demolished in 1746.*

Arthur Bedford is treated briefly by DNB, *slightly by* CBEL, *less by* NCBEL, *and summarily by* Foster, Alumni Oxoniensis, *and* Nichols, Illustrations. *Joseph Wood Krutch,* Comedy and Conscience after the Restoration *(rev. ed., New York, 1949) terms him "an industrious pedant," although Defoe "read him with approval." He was no narrow scholar: he wrote two books intelligently disputing Sir Isaac Newton's* Ancient

PREFACE

Chronology, *made a mark as an orientalist, a critic of modern music, and an astronomer. Late in life he attended Frederick, Prince of Wales, as chaplain, and from 1724 onward was chaplain as well of Ashe's Hospital in Hoxam, where he took up his final residence and died (13 August 1745), aged 78, from the effects of making outdoor observations on the comet of that year.*

Serious Reflections *is reprinted from a copy at Yale (Beinecke Hag 12 2 v.2). It collates A-1⁴(72 pp.), with vertical chainlines.* A Second Advertisement *is reprinted from British Museum 641.e.16 (3), collating B^8, with vertical chainlines. It is mostly uncut at the foot, but all leaves are guarded, slightly affecting a few inner margins. Although Lowe-Arnott-Robinson do not evidently regard this copy as imperfect, it seems almost certainly to lack preliminaries; but I know of no other copy.* The Evil and Danger of Stage-Plays *is reprinted from the Yale copy (Beinecke Haf 21 706b) collating $A^7 B-P^8 Q^4$. In this text $B1^1$ exists in two states, one (cancelled) bearing the inflammatory title "Hell upon Earth, or, the Language of the Play-House," which we print as an appendix from Lowe's copy, now at Harvard (Thr.417.06*).*

PREFACE

It should be noted that neither of the British Museum copies contains this leaf, as Lowe-Arnott-Robinson suggest. A Serious Remonstrance *is reprinted from a copy at Yale (Beinecke Haf 21 7196) collating* $A^4 a^4 b^2 B-Z^8 Aa-Bb^8$ *(440 pp., vertical chainlines).* A Sermon, *1730, is reprinted from British Museum 225.h.11 (2.), collating* π^1 $A-E^4$ *(42 pp., vertical chainlines), compared with Harvard Thr. 417.30*.*

April, 1972   A.F.

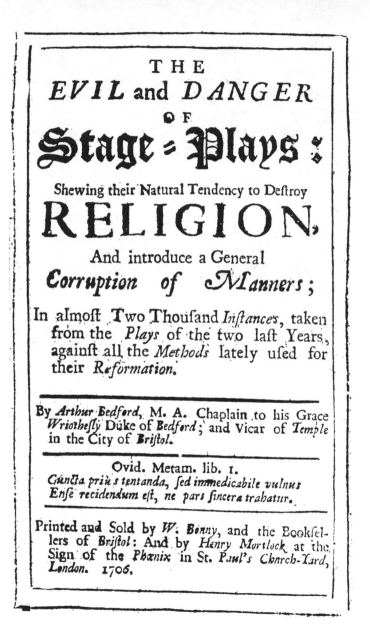

THE
EVIL and *DANGER*
OF
𝕾𝖙𝖆𝖌𝖊 = 𝕻𝖑𝖆𝖞𝖘 :

Shewing their Natural Tendency to Deſtroy

RELIGION,

And introduce a General

Corruption of Manners ;

In almoſt Two Thouſand *Inſtances*, taken from the *Plays* of the two laſt Years, againſt all the *Methods* lately uſed for their *Reformation.*

By *Arthur Bedford*, M. A. Chaplain to his Grace *Wriotheſly* Duke of *Bedford* ; and Vicar of *Temple* in the City of *Briſtol.*

Ovid. Metam. lib. 1.

Cuncta priùs tentanda, ſed immedicabile vulnus Enſe recidendum eſt, ne pars ſincera trahatur.

Printed and Sold by *W. Bonny*, and the Bookſellers of *Briſtol* : And by *Henry Mortlock* at the Sign of the *Phœnix* in St. *Paul's Church-Yard*, *London.* 1706.

TO THE
READER.

I Have endeavoured in the following Sheets, to give a short Account of the Profaneness and Immorality of the English Stage, in the two last Years: And as the eminent Labours of Mr. Collier and others, have justly alarm'd the Nation; so I hope, that my weak Endeavours may be in some Measure serviceable, for their farther Conviction. What the Success hereof will be, I must leave to God, whose Cause it is, and who is oftentimes pleas'd to make Use of mean Instruments, for the Vindication of his Glory. I expect to be reproach'd as others have been, who have gone before me on this Subject; however, I have this Comfort, That I have acted sincerely, and discharged my Conscience herein; and indeed I have thought my self under some solemn Obligations, to set forth

A 2   these

these Devices of Satan in their proper Colours.

First, *As I profess my self to be a* Christian. *I have solemnly promised to* renounce the Devil and all his Works, the Pomps and Vanities of this wicked World, *and all the sinful Lusts of the* Flesh, *and consequently am obliged to oppose those Places, where the Devil is honoured, by* Prayers *to him, and* Praises *of him; where the* Heathen Gods *are adored in all their* Pomp *and* Grandeur; *where* Religion *is undermin'd,* Vice *is encouraged, and more particularly, A-* dultery *and* Whoredom *is pleaded for with all possible Industry*

Secondly, *As I have the Honour to be intrusted by* God *in the Work of the* Ministry. *In this Station I am oblig'd to oppose every thing which is contrary to his Honour, which hath a Tendency to* Atheism, *and to render the* Holy Scriptures *and all revealed Religion contemptible. It hath pleased God to* (a) Ezek. *place me as* (a) *a* Watchman; *I have* 33. 1 to 10. *accordingly given Notice of the Sword approaching,* (i. e.) *of those Methods, which, if not prevented, will provoke* God *to enter into* Judgment. *Whether they who frequent those Places, will take* Warning

Warning *hereby,* or not, *I cannot tell.*
However, I have this Satisfaction ; their
blood muſt be upon their own heads,
if they ſlight it : I have delivered my
own ſoul.

Thirdly, *The actual Building of a*
Play-Houſe *in this City, and their fre-*
quent Actings *near it, as well as at the*
Bath, *hath been another Inducement.*
Theſe Emiſſaries travel from Place to
Place throughout the Land, as if they
deſigned to ſow their Tares in every
Town, and therefore it is high Time to
ſhew the Conſequences thereof. The Ene-
my lay ſometime without our Gates, and is
now come into (b) *the City, in Defiance*   (b) Briſtol.
of the Magiſtrates : And as it hath pleaſed
God *by his* Providence *to place me*
herein ; ſo I thought my ſelf as well as
others, to be more immediately concerned
on this Occaſion.

Having *therefore thus diſcharg'd my*
Duty, I thank God, *I am very eaſy, and*
value not all the Calumnies, Cenſures and
Reproaches, which have been, are, or
may be caſt upon me for the ſame. I
am ſure, that none of theſe things can hurt
me, or deſtroy that inward Peace and
Satisfaction, which is above all outward
Accidents. I know, that the Holy Jeſus

A 3   *was*

was reviled and slandered, and therefore

(c) Matth.
10. 25.

I consider, that (c) It is enough for the disciple that be as his master, and the servant as his lord; and that he saith

(d)Matth.
5. 10.11.12.

(d) Blessed are ye, when men shall revile you, and persecute you, and say all manner of evil against you falsly for my sake; and commands all who thus suffer, to rejoyce and be exceeding glad, because their reward is great in heaven, and thus the Prophets were persecuted, who were in former Ages.

I am the better satisfied, that it is the Cause of God, which I have espoused, because it exposeth such as are engaged therein, to the Censures and Aspersions of wicked Men, and such as scruple no Falsity, when they endeavour to vilify their Adversaries. And I must as freely own, that had it not been his Cause, I was the most unfit Person of any, to be engaged in it. The Poets, whom I deal with, are own'd to be Men of the greatest Parts, Wit and Ingenuity, and can therefore paint over a bad Cause, that its Deformity is not easily discovered. And therefore as these Flashes of Wit, and modern Accomplishments are what I do not affect; so the Success which these my Endeavours may meet with, and the

Good,

Good, which I hope, they may do, ought not in the least to be ascrib'd to me ; but wholly to that God, *(e) who* hath chosen the foolish things of the world, to confound the things which are mighty ; *and who* hath chosen the base things of the world, and things which are despised, yea, and things which are not, to bring to nought things which are, that no flesh should glory in his presence. *I must therefore desire the* Reader, *to pray to* God, *for a Blessing on this Design, to discover these Wiles of* Satan, *and if he finds his Prayers answered, let him give* God *the Glory.*

(e) 1 Cor. 1. 27, 28, 29.

When I first engaged in this Controversy, the common Censure was, that I said more than I could prove. Whether I have proved what I have said let others judge. I might have given larger Proof, if I had not confined my self to so narrow a Compass. However, I hope, that for the Future, when a Clergy Man *preacheth against the* Play-House, *he may be believed, and not be put to the Trouble of proving the same by another Collection.*

Whatever some Men may urge in Vindication of the Stage, I must believe, that the Poets *cannot but in their own Consciences think themselves highly guil-*

A 4   *ty*

ty, and justly censur'd; I am sure, that they are sometimes, tho' seldom, so ingenious, as to confess it. One (f) tells us, that the Poets comply with the People, and therefore they have a Spice of Profaneness, that they rather encourage Vice, by setting it off with a Lustre, than blacken it; and render Virtue rather Folly, than shew the Beauty of it; with much more to the same Purpose. Another (g) denying that the Poets are guilty of the Corruption of Morals, and the Encouraging of Vice, according to the general Complaint against the Stage; yet he is so free as to own, that if in Strictness, this was true, it was enough to justify all the Severity of late express'd against it. As they know their Guilt, so their Perseverance therein is a Sign of the greater Obstinacy, and renders their Cause more inexcusable.

If any Reflection, which I have made seems too severe, I have this Apology; That if the Persons, whom I deal with, were concerned in a Religious Controversy, tho' I had differ'd from them in Opinion, yet I should have been obliged to treat them with all possible Tenderness. But as the blasphemous Language of

the

(f) The Lawyers Fortune, *Pag* 37, *line* 11, &c.

(g) An Act at Oxford, Preface *page* 5.

the Play-House *raiseth the Blood at the Reading therof, so it naturally produces more warm Reflections ; and when there is not so much as a Pretence of Conscience, but the Design is to destroy all* Religion *whatsoever, in such a Case, an harsh Expression, or an harsher Punishment may be more easily excus'd.*

I have in some Places been forced to produce the Quotations at Length, but there are many in the Margin of as gross a Nature ; and tho' I thought my self oblig'd to mention some, which are fitter wholly to be buried in Oblivion, yet I hope that the Reader will think the Antidote to be as strong as the Poison which I have exposed. He therefore who would be a Judge in this Controversy, is desired to turn to the Pages of some Plays, where he may view the Hemlock in its own Soil, and be frequently convinced, that more might be added on this Occasion.

I have taken the best Care, which I could of the Quotations in the Margin, and hope that there are but few Mistakes, either of Page or Line. But if a Quotation should happen to be doubtful, the Reader is desired to view the Design of the Poet in the Lines before, and especially

specially after that which is quoted, by
which Method he may be more fully
convinced, that I have not misrepresented any of the Passages, and where the
Quotations consist of many Lines, I have
mentioned only that, which I have supposed to be the first or second for my
Purpose. If I should mistake in reckon-
ing the Lines of a Page, I suppose
the Comparer will excuse such a Fault,
if he finds the Quotation to be near the
Line which I have mentioned.

The Plays generally consisting of two
Names in the Front of the Title Page,
I have made Choice of the first, except
in that one, call'd Monsieur de Pour-
ceaugnac, or Squire Trelooby. This
the Reader is desired to observe, because there is one Play called The
Faithful General, and another called
The Loyal Subject, or The Faithful
General; and therefore if the Reader
should turn to the wrong Play, he may
think that I am unjust to the Poets,
when the Fault is his and not mine.

I am not conscious that I have injur'd
the Stage by any false Quotation, or
such as will not prove, what they are
quoted for. In this Case he who compares them may easily judge. I have left
out

out some which might have been added, and others which would admit of some slender Apologies, However, Passages which are the least exceptionable, are known and judg'd from their Confederates, and the Design of the whole. I think it needless to add more, since the Tenth Part of what I have quoted, is sufficient to prove, that our Poets are the Bane of Religion, the Promoters of Vice, and the Nuisance of the Nation.

THE

THE
Contents.

CHAP.

The CONTENTS.

THE

THE
EVIL and *DANGER*
OF
Stage=Plays.

CHAP. I.

The Obstinacy of the Stage.

THE *English Stage* taking a Liberty unknown in any *Heathen*, and notoriously *Scandalous* in a *Christian* Country, Mr. *Jeremy Collier* first began the *Attack* against them, in his Book, intituled, *A Short View of the English Stage*; wherein he fully convicted the *Poets* of *Immodesty* and *Profaneness,*

B

faneneſs, Curſing, Swearing, Encouraging of *Vice*, Diſcouraging of *Virtue*, Abuſe of the Holy Scriptures, with ſeveral other *Notorious Crimes*, deſtructive to *Chriſtianity*, and tending to ſubvert the *Principles* of all *Religion*, and the *Notions* of *Good* and *Evil*. This Book met with a deſerv'd Eſteem from ſuch who had a *Zeal* for *God's Glory*, and a *Deſire* to ſuppreſs *Vice*, and promote *Virtue*. They had afterward a truer Senſe of the *Abominations* of the *Play-Houſe*, and did accordingly oppoſe, abhor and deteſt the ſame. When its Intereſt thus declin'd, it was expected that the *Poets would* have *reform'd* their *Plays*, and by this *Method* cut off all future *Objections*; but inſtead thereof, they only excuſe themſelves and their paſt *Behaviour*. Indeed Mr. *Dryden*, a Man of the greateſt Parts and Wit among them, was ſenſible that their *Cauſe* was too bad to be defended, and therefore would not attempt an *Impoſſibility*; but Mr. *Collier*, equally expoſing ſome *Plays* written by Mr. *Congreve*, and Mr. *Dennis*, and ſuch as juſtly deſerv'd the higheſt Cenſure, they were willing to waſh the *Black-Moor* white, and endeavoured to vindicate

HELL upon EARTH:

OR THE

LANGUAGE

OF THE

Play-House.

CHAP I.

The Obstinacy of the Stage.

THE *English Stage* taking a Liberty unknown in any *Heathen*, and notoriously *Scandalous* in a *Christian* Country, Mr. *Jeremy Collier* first began the *Attack* against them, in his Book, intituled, *A Short View of the English Stage* ; wherein he fully con-victed their *Poets* of *Immodesty* and *Pro-*

B   *faneness,*

fanenes, *Cursing*, *Swearing*, *Encouraging of Vice*, *Discouraging of Virtue*, *Abuse of the Holy Scriptures*, with several other *Notorious Crimes*, destructive to *Christianity*, and tending to subvert the *Principles* of all *Religion*, and the *Notions* of *Good* and *Evil*. This Book met with a deserv'd Esteem from such who had a *Zeal* for *God's Glory*, and a *Desire* to suppress *Vice*, and promote *Virtue*. They had afterward a truer Sense of the *Abominations* of the *Play-House*, and did accordingly oppose, abhor and detest the same. When its Interest thus declin'd, it was expected that the *Poets* would have *reform'd* their *Plays*, and by this *Method* cut off all future *Objections*; but instead thereof, they only endeavour to vindicate their past *Behaviour*. Indeed Mr. *Dryden*, a Man of the greatest Parts and Wit among them, was sensible that their *Cause* was too bad to be defended, and therefore would not attempt an *Impossibility*; but Mr. *Collier*, equally exposing some *Plays* written by Mr. *Congreve*, and Mr. *Dennis*, and such as justly deserv'd the highest Censure, they were willing to wash the *Black-Moor* white, and endeavour'd to vindi-

cate

cate themselves and the *Play-House.*
The weakness of their Arguments, occasioned by the Badness of their Cause,
gave Mr. *Collier* an Opportunity not
only for a farther Confutation, but also to shew the unfair Dealing of both
these *Authors,* and to satisfy the World,
that he undertook no more than what
he was able to prove to the Shame of his
Adversaries. Besides Mr. *Collier's* Endeavours, Sir *Richard Blackmoor,* and
others, attempted also in Print to *correct* and *reform* the *scandalous Abuses*
and *Disorders* of the *Stage,* and turn
the *Poetry* of this Nation into another
Channel; but all Efforts were found
too unsuccesful. Instead of a *Reformation,* Satan muster'd up all his *Posse*;
the Apprehension that his *Great Diana*
was despis'd, and his *Temples* in *Danger of being destroy'd,* set his Engins
at work to plead his Cause: And it is
very observable, that as they wanted
Arguments, so they endeavour'd to supply that Defect with *Railing* and *Scurrility.*

The *Press* being thus employ'd *Pro*
and *Con,* had only this Effect, to satisfy a great Part of the Nation, where
the *Original* of our *Atheism, Profane-*

ness

ness and *Debauchery* lay; but it could produce no farther *Reformation.* Accordingly some Gentlemen in the City of *London,* who were *zealous* for the *Glory of God,* and the *suppressing* of *Immorality* and *Profaneness,* resolv'd upon another *Method.* In the Year 1699 they prosecuted several of the *Players* in the Court of *Common Pleas,* upon the *Statute* of 3 *Jac.* 1. for profanely using the *Name of God* upon the *Stage,* and obtain'd *Verdicts* against them. Afterward in *Easter Term* 1701, the *Players* belonging to the *House* in *Little Lincolns-Inn-Fields* were indicted at the *King's-Bench Bar,* before the *Right Honourable* the *Lord Chief Justice Holt,* for using several *scandalous Expressions,* to be seen in their *Plays* call'd, *Love for Love, The Provok'd Wife,* &c. at which Time several of the *Actors* were brought in Guilty by the *Jury,* without going from the *Bar,* the *Evidence* against them being so full and plain.

The Success of this Attempt was little more than that of the former. The *Players* had before found out a *Method* (as they thought) to avoid the *Penalty* of the *Law,* and yet retain the *Sins*; which was by putting the Word *Gad* instead

instead of *God*, and *Lard* instead of *Lord*, in a Profane and Contemptible Manner. If they must not swear *By the Name of God* (of which in the next Chapter) they will endeavour to make his *Name* ridiculous, and rather than avoid one S*in* be guilty of another. However, this is now their constant *Method*, and thinking themselves secure, they retain all the *Swearing, Cursing, Blasphemy,* and *Profaneness* which they had before.

When these Endeavours were ineffectual, and they who aim'd at the *Glory of God* had only this Satisfaction that they had discharg'd their *Duty*; the *Actors* little regarded the Laws of *Man*, and at the same Time loudly cry'd to *God* himself for Judgments in their *Plays* call'd, *The Tempest*, and *Mackbeth*, wherein they presume to imitate the *Almighty* in his wonderful Acts; wherein they ascribe the *Lightnings, Thunder, Storm* and *Tempest* to the Force of *Magical Arts,* that the *Hearers* might think them to be no Judgments from *God*: And thus they mock'd the *Great Governour* of the World, *who alone commands the winds and the seas, and they obey him.* However, *God* pleaded his own Cause,

B 3 and

and shew'd us that he would not be thus affronted, by sending a most dreadful Storm on the 26th Day of *November* 1703, which fill'd us with Horror and Amazement ; wherein he manifested his Anger and his Power, and made us sensible to our Sorrow, That *this was his hand, and he did it.* And yet so great was the *Profaneness* of the *Stage* under such signal Judgments, that we are told [*a*] *the Actors did in a few Days after, entertain again their Audience with these Ridiculous Plays*; and that *at the mention of the Chimneys* [*b*] *being blown down* (Mackbeth, page 20.) *the Audience were pleas'd to Clap at an unusual Length of Pleasure and Approbation*; as if they were all agreed to outbrave the Judgment, throw *Providence* out of the Chair, and place the *Devil* in his stead : As if they would set *God* again at Defiance, and provoke him to vindicate his Honour, in sending a greater Calamity upon us.

[*a*] A Representation of the Impiety and Immorality of the *English Stage.* Page 5.
[*b*] Mr. *Collier's* Dissuasive from the *Play-House.* Page 15.

To this I may add, That the *Plays* call'd, *The Tempest,* and *Mackbeth,* are now far outdone by a later which was printed in this Year, call'd, *The British Enchanters*; The *Scene* is [*] *England,* and consequently our Nation, re-

[*] *Dramatis Personæ in fine.*

[c] represented as wholly addicted to Diabolical Practices. The Design is, I think, to recommend the Study of *Magick*, and he who can patiently see and hear the one, hath made a great Step toward the Practice of the other. Here we have [d] Enchantments with [e] Rods to make the better Jest of the [f] *Sacred Story*: And lest others should not know how to make a Compact with the *Devil*, and ruin their Souls to all Eternity, this [g] *Blasphemous Sentence* is spoken for their Imitation.

> *See it perform'd——And thou shalt be,*
> *Dire Instrument of Hell, a God to me.*

[c] *The Stage Beaux toss'd in a Blanket.* page 23. line 31. If the *Scene* be among *Christians*, I think it should be avoided only for the scandalizing of the weak; and I take the Poet to be inculpable, since he only draws from the Practice of the World. [d] *Page* 1.

line 4. p. 4. in fine. p. 16. [e] *Page* 1. in fine. [f] *Exod.* 7. 11, 12. [g] *Page* 12. line 22.

Here we have *Devils* with [h] Instruments of Horror, some rising from under the *Stage*, others flying down from above; some [i] singing, and others [k] playing upon *Musick*; some [l] dancing and others [m] attending on their *Enchanters*; some [n] rang'd in order of Battle, and others [o] fighting in the Air. Here we have [p] Hell

[h] *Page* 16. line 15, &c. page 33. [i] *Page* 23. line penult. [k] *Page* 33. [l] *Page* 24. line 8. [m] *Page* 24. line 22. [n] *Page* 33.

[o] *Page* 33, 34. [p] *Page* 22. line 11. He who peruseth this Quotation, is desir'd to compare it with *Prov.* 21. 16. and Mr. *Mede's* Discourse upon it, *page* 31.

B 4

re-

represented as a Jest, with *Men* and *Women* chain'd in Rows, and [q] *Devils* for their Companions; nay, carrying a *Man* to the Place of *Torments*, with a *Flourish of Musick sounding Triumph*, in direct Opposition to (*) *the Joy of Angels* at a Sinner's Conversion. Here we have the dreadful Judgments of the *Almighty* mock'd, such as [r] *Thunder* and [s] *Lightning*, and also [t] *Raining of Fire from Heaven*, as *God* formerly overthrew *Sodom* and *Gomorrah*: And all this is perform'd in the *Play-House* lately built (as they tell us) for *Reformation*.

When the *Actors* imitated the *Tempest* in jest, we afterward felt it in earnest: I pray *God* to divert the same for the future, together with that more dismal Calamity, which they so loudly call for.

When *Her Majesty* was graciously pleas'd on that sad Occasion of the *Storm*, to appoint a Day of *Publick Fasting* and *Humiliation*, most of the *Bishops*, and *Clergy* of the City of *London* did then in their Sermons preach particularly against the *Notorious Profaneness* of the *Play-Houses*; and when they had thus discharg'd their Duty, they could not but hope, That the Attacking the *Stage* from the *Pulpit* as well

[q] *Page* 20. *line* 10.

(*) *Luke* 15. 10.

[r] *Page* 1. *line* 5. and *antepenult.* *p.* 33. *l.* 19.

[s] *Page* 16. *line* 19. *p.* 34. *l.* 8.

[t] *Page* 33. *line* 38.

well as from the *Press* (if it did not teach them *Religion*) would have taught them better *Manners*; but the Effect was only this, These *Watchmen have delivered their own souls.*

About this Time *Her Majesty* was pleas'd to send Her strict and solemn [*u*] *Order*, prohibiting, not only whatever was *offensive on the* Stage, but also *all other Disorders and ill Customs*; *such as admitting Vizard Masks, and Gentlemen's going behind the* Scenes, *&c.* which *Order*, according to *Royal Direction*, was read before the *Audience* (for they did not dare to do otherwise) and after that, both the *Order* and the *Actor*, who read it, were hiss'd off from the *Stage.* When I first read this, I must confess, I ceas'd to wonder that the lesser Efforts were insignificant, since they were grown to that Height of Impudence, as to insult even the *Royal Authority*, to dare *Her sacred Majesty*, to contemn Her pious Care, and so visibly to affront Her.

At the Time of the *Fast* abovementioned, there was printed a *small Treatise*, intitul'd, *A Representation of the Impiety and Immorality of the* English *Stage*, giving an Account of their Prosecution for *Profane, Lewd,* and *Atheistical*

[*u*] A Letter in Answer to some Queries relating to the *Stage, page* 20.

istical Expressions, and a *Catalogue* of
several others spoken since, to shew
that they continu'd as *obstinate* as ever:
The Design hereof was to disswade
such as had any Sense of *Religion* from
frequenting these Nurseries of *Atheism*
and *Licentiousness*. Mr. *Collier* also
printed *A Disswasive from the Play-
House* at the same Time.

   These *Methods* made the *Poets* angry,
but could not reform them. [*x*] *They*
(*x*) *Jer.* 5. *have made their faces harder than a rock,*
3.   *and they have refused to return.* One
Quotation out of the *Play*, call'd, *An
Act at Oxford*, in the *Epistle Dedicatory*, *pag.* 8. may serve at present to shew
their Spleen. *Mr.* Collier (saith the
Author) *thought the Proclamation against
Irreligion, and Her Majesty's Regulation of the Theatres imperfect as his Works*
(indeed he might think it insufficient
when it was hiss'd off from the *Stage*)
*therefore on the Fast Day out comes his
supplemental Pamphlet, to rectify the Go-
vernments Omissions.* ——— *Had he been*
*content with the Countenance the World
gave his* View, *and gone no farther, it
might have pass'd for a Discourse wrote
in the Cause of Religion; but his and
his Associates Conduct since shews, there's
another Cause on Foot.* A pretty Turn !
                           Her

Her *Majesty's* Order is hiss'd at, Her pious Care contemn'd, and contrary to Her Intention, they go on in Sin the more securely; looking on it as a Disrespect to Her, for any other to assist Her in Her *Pious Designs.* This *Author* is pleas'd to look on it as an *Affront* to Her *Majesty,* to think Her *Regulations* not sufficient; and yet in the same *Play* he is guilty of [*y*] *Swearing, Cursing, Exposing the Universities, and Societies for Reformation, the Aldermen and Officers, Marriage and Religion* it self, and pleads for *Pimping* and *Whoring;* and that Her *Majesty* may proceed no farther, he gives fair Warning (tho' in respectful Terms) that the *Regulating* of the *Play-House* may occasion a *Rebellion.*

(*y*) See the following Chapters in this Book.

However, the Attempts for a *Reformation* did not stop here; Her *Majesty* was afterward graciously pleas'd by *Letters Patents,* dated the 14*th* of *December, Ann.* 1705, to authorize *John Vanbrugh* and *William Congreve* Esqs; to ininto the *Plays, for the better Reforming the Abuses and Immorality of the Stage,* and take care that nothing should be acted to the Prejudice of *Religion* and *Good Manners,* and consequently to be accountable for all future Misbehaviours.

After

After all these Endeavours for a *Reformation* of the *Play-House*, by Her *Gracious Majesty*, the *Judges*, the *Bishops*, the *Clergy* and the *Laity*, from the *Courts of Judicature*, the *Pulpit* and the *Press*; it is Time to enquire, Whether the Effects have answer'd their Expectation? The *Actors* on, and *Frequenters* of the *Stage*, tell us, with a Confidence peculiar to themselves, That they are wonderfully *Reform'd* of late; and by this Pretence they think to impose on such as do not frequent them. But this is only a *Sham* to deceive the World.

For *First*, They cannot be *reform'd* of late, since they frequently *act* the old *Plays*, and even such as are most notoriously rampant and scandalous. They ought to [z] *purge out the old leaven, that they may be a new lump.* When Mr. *Power* and his *Company* came to *Bristol*, he urg'd this Plea, That he would *Act* nothing, but what should be sober and modest, *&c.* and express'd a great Esteem which he had for Mr. *Collier's* Works, and Design to *reform* the *Stage*; and that he only selected the best *Plays*, and most inoffensive. This was a fine Pretence. But yet he *acted* near that City, on *Monday July* the

[z] 1 *Cor.* 5. 7.

the 23d, 1705, the *Comedy*, call'd, *Love for Love*; and on *Monday* the 13th of *August* following, he acted *The Provok'd Wife*, he himself (as I was inform'd) taking the Part of Sir *John Brute*, the *Provoking Husband*, which was the most *scandalous*, *profane* and *atheistical* Part of the whole *Play*; tho' it is remarkable that both these *Plays* have been evidently censur'd by Mr. *Collier*, both in his *Short View of the Stage*, and *Reply* in its Vindication; and the *Players* in *Little Lincolns-Inn-Fields* were found guilty in the *King's Bench*, and fin'd for the *Acting* of them.

Hence it appears that we cannot believe a Word which they say for themselves; the Examples of Justice will not cause them to beware: And as they are taught by the *Father of Lies*, so they are apt Scholars, for they scruple no such *Sin* to serve their Turn.

Secondly, They vindicate all their past Behaviour, and cry out publickly against a *Reformation*. When the *Clergy* upon the *Fast Day* preach'd against the *Stage*, there was also a *Book* printed, intitul'd, *Concio Laici*, or the *Lay Man's Sermon*; endeavouring to prove,

That

That *Hypocrisy,* more than open *Lewd-*
ness, is the crying Sin of this Nation, and
brought that dreadful Storm upon us.
The *Author* complains, That *the Clergy*
preach not against Hypocrisy (an impudent and false Assertion) and gives his

[*a*] Page 7. Reason, [*a*] That *tho' Hypocrisy is a Foe*
to Religion ; yet the *Author* thinks he
may confidently affirm, that *it is a*
Friend to the Church : But then he gives
this Caution, *Remember I speak of no*
particular Church, but of every Church
whatsoever. Like to this is that of [*b*]

[*b*] Absalom Mr. *Dryden* ;
and Achito-
phel.

For Priests of all Religions are the same.

It is easy to prove, That in the *Lan-*
guage of the *Play-House,* *Hypocrisy* now
consists either in writing against the
Stage, or putting the Laws in Execution against *Immorality* and *Profaneness.*
It seems therefore (according to this *Au-*
thor's Opinion) that there was a Design
of *Reformation* carry'd on, and this
made *God* angry ; but had we been *pro-*
fane, he had been better pleas'd. We
had a Shew of *Religion,* and abhorr'd
the *Abominations* of the *Play-House,* and
this occasion'd such dreadful Judgments.
This

This was *horrid Language* as a Preparation for a *Fast*, and not to be parallel'd by *Jezebel* her self.

No *Clergy* Man will vindicate *Hypocrisy*, and perhaps there are none who do not preach against it.   But that such Pamphlets should appear at such a Time, is very surprising, and beyond the *Pagan Examples*.   The Gilding over such Notions cannot hide the *Blasphemy*; since the true *English* thereof, is this: *If you endeavour to reform the Vices of the Age, you provoke God to be angry; but if you let Men alone to live as they list, it will divert the Judgment*.   All Religion must down; since *Atheists* are fittest for these Mens Purposes.   *Good God*! What a degenerate Age do we live in ? Here are Men, who not only *think wickedly, that God is such a one as themselves;* but dare to publish their Thoughts, as a better Direction to observe the *Fast*.   Accordingly the *Author* gives a Character of such, who put the Laws in Execution against *Prophaneness*, [*c*] that they are *Persons who are* either [*c*] *Page* 25. *vehement for Reforming all the World but themselves, and allow themselves in Diabolical Crimes, as Extortion, Fraud, Oppression, Malice and Slander, but are*

highly

*highly offended at Human Vices, and
Human Frailties in others : Or else, [d]
are only offended at Vice in others, be-*
[d] Page 26. *cause they would erect a Monopoly for it
themselves.* Here were fine *Methods* to
turn all the *Preaching* on the *Fast Day*
into Contempt, to affront the *Queen*
who appointed the *Fast* to be observ'd
because of the *National Sins,* and expose the *Bishops* who compil'd the *Lit-
turgy* for, and preach'd on that Occasion.

The *Stage* being attack'd from the
Press, and the *Poets* finding themselves
unable publickly to vindicate their
Cause, take another *Method.* In their
Printed Plays they add *Prefaces* in Vindication of *Plays* in General, and frequently insert in their *Acts* some Speeches to this Purpose. This *Method* they
conclude will Influence their *Hearers,*
make them Proof against all other Arguments, and keep them firm to their
Interest. This they cannot but think
most effectual, because it is not proba-
ble, at least not fit, that the *Plays*
should come into the Hands of any, but
such as are delighted with them. This
was their subtle Policy to maintain
their Ground, in Hope of an Opportunity

tunity to enlarge their Conquests. Beside these Scraps which we find in their
Plays, there was one *acted* and printed
wholly on this *Subject*, intitul'd, *The Stage
Beaux toss'd in a Blanket*, or *Hypocrisy
Alamode.* The Design of it was to
expose Mr. *Collier*, and the *Play* it self
is stuff'd with *Scurrility, Lies, Swearing* and *Cursing*, the common Garnish
of our modern *Poetry*. I shall not at
present trouble the Reader with any
Quotations out of the *Play* it self, being all of a Piece : The *Drama* imme-
diatly before the *first Act*, hath shewn the
Poet's fine *Language*, good *Breeding* and
Manners, excellent *Morality*, and great
Regard to the Ninth-Commandment. In
this *Drama* the *Poet* gives us this Character of Sir *Jerry Witwood* (and all
the World knows who he means) that
he is a [e] *Pert, Talkative, Half-wit-
ted Coxcomb*, [f] *vain of a very little
Learning, always swims with the Stream
of Popular Opinion, a great Censurer both
of Men and Books, always positive seldom or never in the right, a noisy Pretender to Virtue, and an impudent Pretender
to Modesty, an Hypocrite, and false Zealot
for Religion, and sets up for a Reformer of
the Stage, of a sagacious Nose in finding*

[e] *Jude v:*
9. 1 *Pet.* 2
23. *Matth.* 11.
29. *Rom.* 12.
21. *Matth.* 7.
3, 4, 5.
[f] *Eph.*
4. 25.

C
out

out *Smut* or *Obscenity* ; *a wonderful Ar-*
tist at extracting Profaneness out of all
things that fall into his Hands ; *a pro-*
fess'd Enemy of the Stage, tho' a Frequen-
ter of it ; *once thought a Divine, but for*
Reasons best known to himself, he hath
cast off his Gown for the Vanities of a
Beau Wigg and Sword ; *vain, proud, ill*
[g]*Matth.* *natur'd, and* [g] *uncapable of Conver-*
7. 1, 2. *sion.* Let the Texts in the *Margin* shew
how agreeable their Practice is to the
Example of *Christ*, and the Rules of
Christianity, and let the Reader guess
at the same time, concerning the gen-
teel Behaviour which they so much
pretend to. However, this is the least.
The *Prologue* exposes *Religion* in a *Satyr*
pretended to be levell'd against the *Dis-*
senters ; and the *Epilogue* is as bitter
against the *Societies* for *Reformation*.
As for *Profaneness*, this *Play* is like the
Rest. To transcribe the whole would
be *horrid*, and therefore let the Reader
guess at it, from these two Lines in the
Prologue.

A Pox upon their Zeal to save our Souls
They'd make us honest, that's they'd mak
                              (us Fool

Wh:

What *Language* can be more *Diabolical?* or with what Confidence can such pretend they are reform'd, when *Lucifer* could scarcely speak so daring? Here is dreadful *Cursing*, a *Satyr* upon *Zeal*, *Piety* and *Honesty*, to divert their *Hearers*, stifle their *Consciences*, destroy *Religion*, and teach the *Language* of *Hell*. This is contain'd in a short Rhyme to be remembred the better: And here we see the Effects of their pretended *Reformation*.

However, As the *Actors* were found guilty in *Westminster-Hall* of *profane Expressions*; so there is an Alteration in their *Plays*, tho' not for the better. They now set themselves in direct Opposition to *Justice*, a Crime which they dar'd not to be guilty of in former Ages. Accordingly in [b] their *Plays* they represent the *Magistrates* by [i] *ridiculous Names*, as such who live by *Extortion* and *Connivance*, expose them as guilty of [k] *Whoredom*, [l] as exposing themselves, and the rest of the *Bench*, (m) as talking *Smut*, and in love with young Girls, (n) as receiving of *Bribes* and, for the sake thereof, excusing gross Offenders, but severely punishing such as have nothing to pay. Thus they make

[b] *The Humour of the Age: A* Comedy. 1703.
[i] *Drama.*
[k] *Page* 6. *line* 22.
[l] *Page* 14. *and* 16.
[m] *Page* 15, *and* 43.
[n] *Page* 38. *and* 7.

C 2 the

the *Magistrates* the Jest of the *Stage,*
(o) Page 7. and (o) send them away with a dishonourable *Exit;* and this they represent,
as *The Humour of the Age.* This is a
constant Affront, which they now put
upon the *Judges, Aldermen, Juries,
Informers,* and all such as endeavour
to *reform* the *Corruptions* either of the
Nation or the *Play-House.* Others are
afraid of *Justice,* these bid it Defiance:
Others pay a respect to Magistrates,
these despise them: And certainly this
is a great *Obligation* for the Future,
as well as a *Reformation* from what is
past.

However the Notion of a *Reformation* is something to amuse the World,
and what they think will promote their
Interest, and therefore they have of late
pretended much thereto. The *Play-
House* in the *Hay-Market* is said to be
built only to *reform* the *Stage,* and
what Effects Time will bring forth
may be guess'd at from the *Prologue*
spoken at its first Opening, which is
notoriously *scandalous* and *profane* with-
(p) Line 1. out Excuse. The (p) *Builder* is compar'd to *God,* and the *Building* to the
Creation of the World.

Such

Such was our Builder's Art, that soon as (q) nam'd,
This Fabrick, like the Infant World, was fram'd.

(q) Gen. 1. 3, 6, 9, 11, 14, 15, 20, 24, 26, 29.

No Jest serves the Turn like a Droll upon the *Scriptures*; since thereby they are the less regarded at another Time. Besides, it was the Ambition of the fall'n *Angels* to affect a Likeness with God, for which they were turn'd out of *Heaven*; and yet (I think) the *Poet* exceeds that in the following Lines.

The Architect must on dull Order wait ;
But 'tis the Poet only can create.

Had he said, *God and the Poet only can create,* it had been more modest ; for then the *supream Being* had been join'd as a Partner with the *Poets* Abilities, whereas now he is totally excluded as dull and insignificant.

This *Horrid Blasphemy* is so rank, as to raise the Blood at the Reading thereof, and yet Mr. *Estcourt* inserts it, as a choice Quotation, in the *Title* of his Comedy, call'd *The Fair Example.* However, to do this *Gentleman* Justice: When he affected a greater than *Luci-*

C 3 *ferian*

ferian Pride, and attributed the Works of *God* to the *Poet*, and consequently to himself, he did well to omit his *Christian Name*, and write Mr.

Another thing remarkable in this *(r) Line 13.* *Prologue* is the (r) reflecting on *Religion*, and consequently preferring the *Plays* before it.

In the good Age of ghostly Ignorance,
How did Cathedrals rise, and Zeal ad-
(vance ?

The meaning is this. When the World was ignorant Men built *Churches*, and there paid their Devotion to *God*; but now they have more Knowledge, they build *Play-Houses*, and resort to their *Acts*. The Effects of Knowledge are better than the Effects of Ignorance.

(s) Line 19. *(s) For now that pious Pageantry's no more,*
And Stages thrive as Churches did before.

Besides, when they built *Churches*, it was a tedious, and (as we say) a *Church* work. St. *Paul's* hath been a great while in building, and is not yet finished, but the *Play-House* is quickly done.

(t)

(*t*) ———— ———— *soon as nam'd*   (*t*) Line 1.
This Fabrick like the Infant World was
                  fram'd.

And consequently there is another sly Insinuation, that as their Building went on faster; so their Cause is better. *Religion* is the great Enemy to the *Play-Houses*, and therefore their utmost Efforts are to batter it down and destroy it.

In this *Prologue* the Women who frequent the *Play-House* are represented as *Goddesses*, the *Lightning* of their Eyes is fiercer than that of *Jove* or *God* himself, and brighter than the *Sun*. Such Expressions, however gilded over, I take to be *Blasphemy*, and such as cannot be excus'd by any *Hyperbole*; since what (*u*) St. *John* said of *Heav'n*, (*u*) *Rev.* 21. 23. *God* and *Christ* seems here to be applied to the *Play-House*, the *Women* and the *Actors.*

The Lion is known by his Paw, and from this *Prologue* we may guess at the design'd *Reformation*.

However, since there is great Expectation (*x*) from Mr. *Congreves* Abilities and his Care, I shall take Notice of the Improvement of the *Stage* since his *Inspection*.

(*x*) *Parturiunt montes, nascetur ridiculus mus.* Horat de Arte Poetica.

C 4   The

(y) Page. 4.
line 6, 16.
p. 23. l. an-
te-penult. p.
52. l. 27. p.
55. l. 4. p.
56. l, 1. p.
57. l. 14.
(z) Page 4.
line 3, 22
p. 7. l. 22.
p. 33. l. 26.
p. 45. l.19,
32. p. 52. l.
12, 14. p.
63. l. 12.
p. 67. l. pen-
ult.
(a) Page 25.
line 24. p.
29. l. 9. p.
31. l. 1, 32.
p. 45. l. pe-
nult. p. 54. l.
30, 35. p. 68.
l. 17. p. 69.
l. 7.
(b) Page 53.
(c) Page 24,
25, &c.
(d) Page 62,
and 66.
(e) Page 26.
line 25, &c.
p. 29. l. 1,
&c.
(f) Page 28.

The *First* of these *Reform'd Plays* was *The Gamester*, design'd to expose this *Vice*, and consequently to aim at a *Reformation* of *Manners*; at least to impose upon the World, and make them think so. In this *Play* the *Devil* is invok'd in the *first Line* (a very good Beginning) and in (y) *seven* other Places. There are several Instances of (z) *profane Swearing*, and (a) *Cursing.* The (b) fine *Angelica* is dress'd in Mens *Cloaths*, as a Jest upon *Deut.* 23. 5. and *Valere* the *Gamester*, having (c) first pretended a *Reformation*, and broken his solemn Vows, is upon the (d) second Pretence, less solemn than the former (only by the *Poet* suppos'd to be real) rewarded with this fine *Lady* and *Ten Thousand Pounds*, and makes an honourable *Exit*, without any Penance: He loseth his Estate by *Gaming*, and represented as the only Man of Figure and Success. However, if we grant that *Gaming* is expos'd, yet the beforementioned *Vices* are rather promoted.

In the *Comedy* call'd *The Quacks*, a *Smutty Epilogue* is forbid to be spoken, however Care is taken to publish it from the *Press*; but yet there is a Tincture of the (e) same Ingredient, and (f) a *Smutty*

Smutty Song, where the Force of the *Musick* doubles the *Mischief.* Hence our *Monthly Collections* supply the *Singing Masters* to teach the *Ladies* for their farther Improvement. The whole is a *Love Intreague,* and yet this *Play* is as inoffensive as any modern *Comedy.*

But that the World may better judge of these *Abominations,* I shall give some Account of these *Plays* which were printed in the Years 1704, and 1705 until the *Tenth Day* of *March* last ; and whenever I quote any other, I shall place in the Margin the Year in which it was printed. By this, I suppose, it will appear that the half of this Wickedness hath not been publickly Discover'd ; and tho' I do not pretend to cite all exceptionable Passages, yet I believe I shall produce sufficient to prove the *Stage* to be a *Sink of Sin,* a *Cage of Uncleanness,* and the Original Cause of all our Profaneness ; directly tending to root out all *Religion,* contemn the Laws of *God* and *Man,* and affront such as pay a Regard to either.

C H A P.

CHAP. II.

The Stage guilty of Swearing, and Blaf-
phemy.

THat I may the better fet forth our
prefent *Stage* in its proper Colours, I look no farther back, than the
two laft Years; and fhew how directly contrary the Practice thereof is to
the Precepts, and Examples recorded
in the *Holy Scriptures*; and the firft Inftances that I fhall give are their *pro-*
fane Swearing and Blafphemy.

(a) Exod. 20. *Profane Swearing* is a Sin fo direct-
7. *Deut.*5.11. ly forbidden by *God* that (*a*) the *third*
Commandment feems chiefly levell'd a-
gainft it; where we are told that *God*
will not hold them guiltlefs, who fhall of-
fend in this particular. In the *old Law,*
(b) Levit. 5. he who (*b*) fwore ignorantly, or una-
4. wares was guilty, and (*c*) he alfo who
(c) Levit 5. heard it, and conceal'd the Crime.
1. The *Prophets* look'd on this as one
(d) Jer. 23. Caufe of their Calamity. (*d*) *Becaufe*
10. *Hof.* 4. *of Swearing the Land did mourn, and*
2, 7. *the pleafant Places of the Wildderneſs*
(e) Zech. 5. *were dried up.* And when (*e*) *Zecha-*
3. *riah* faw *a flying roll* typifying *the Curfe*
of

of God, he was told that it should destroy every one who was guilty of
Swearing. When our *Blessed Saviour*
expounded the *Law*, he commanded
us (*f*) *not to swear at all; but let our* (f) *Matth. 5.*
Communication be yea, yea, and nay, nay, 34, 37.
since whatsoever is more than these ἐκ τȢ
πονηρȢ ἐςι, *cometh from the Devil:* and
St. *James* above all things cautions us
against it (*g*) *lest we fall into condem-* (g) *Jam. 5.*
nation. And to prevent any Freedom 12.
with such Expressions as have any re-
semblance of *Oaths*, (*h*) Our *Saviour* (h) *Mat.* 12,
tells us, That *of every idle word which* 36, 37.
men shall speak they shall give an account
at the day of judgment. For by our
words we shall be justified, and by our
words we shall be condemned.

Blasphemy is also a *Sin* of that heinous
Nature, that it is reckon'd to be the
Crime, which the *damn'd* in *Hell* are
guilty of, and which makes them un- (i) *Matth.* 12.
capable of Recovery. All other *Sins* 31. *Mark* 3.
are pardonable, but one *Species* of this *Luke* 12. 10.
Sin (*i*) will never be forgiven. It is (k) *Colos.* 3.
positively forbidden in the (*k*) new 8.
Testament, as well as in the old, as (*l*) a 19, 20. *Mark*
Sin which defiles a man. It is a (*m*) Vice 7. 21, 22, 23.
peculiar to the worst of Times, and (m) 2 *Tim.*
(*n*) to the most notorious Sinners. It 3. 1, 2.
 (n) *Rev.* 13.
caus'd 1, 6, 7.

(o) *Act.* 13.
45, 46. *Act.*
18. 6.
(p) *Isai.* 52.
5, 6, and 65.
7. *Ezek.* 35.
12, 13 14, 15.
Rev. 2. 9.
(q) *Lev.* 24.
16.
(r) *Lev.* 24.
11, 12, 13, 14.
(s) 1 *King* 21.
10, 13. *Mat.*
26. 65, 66.
Matth 14. 63.
64. *Acts* 6. 11,
13. and 7. 57,
58.

caus'd (o) the *Apostles* to depart from the *Jews*, and *go to the Gentiles* ; and *God* grant that it may not remove the Light of the *Gospel* from us, as it did from them. It is a *Vice* which *God* (p) particularly resents, which (q) he commanded should be punished with Death ; and accordingly a Capital Punishment was constantly inflicted by the *Jews* on such as were convicted either (r) truly, or (s) falsly of this Crime.

The Sins of *Swearing* and *Blasphemy* are contrary to the first Petition in the *Lord's Prayer*, wherein we daily pray to *God* that his *Name* may *be hallowed* or sanctified among us : They are contrary to the *Creed*, since such who are guilty must either believe, that there is no *God* at all, or else that he is not *Almighty*; but unable to inflict the Penalty, which he hath so solemnly denounced against these *Sins*, in the third *Commandment*.

In short, The *Name* of *God* is so sacred, that it ought not to be mention'd but with a suitable Reverence and Devotion.

(t) *Non vacat exiguis rebus adesse Jovi Ovid.*

(t) *Jupiter*, the Heathen Deity, was represented as one who could not attend on Trifles ; and we debase the *Great Creator* of *Heav'n* and *Earth*, when

when he is (*k*) mention'd in the paltry Concerns of the *Stage* especially in *Comedies*, where they make it their Business to render every thing ridiculous, and whence they banish whatsoever hath a Tendency to a grave or serious Thought; and therefore all such Expressions might properly be omitted by our Modern *Poets*; especially when they (*l*) place the *Gad* instead of *God*, and (*m*) *Lard* instead of *Lord*, in a foppish, drolling, fantastical, and ridiculous Manner, and in a (*n*) Dialect,

(*k*) The Careless Husband, *Page* 4. *line* 18, 25. *p.* 37. *l.* 19, 20. *p.* 55. *L* 2, 3. The Confederacy, *page* 32. *line ult. p.* 61. *l.* 5. The Northern Lass, *p.* 17. *l.* 15. *p.* 19. *l.* 14. *p.* 23. *l.* 28. The Roving Husband reclaim'd, *page* 10. *line* 25. *p.* 11. *l.* 9. The Stage Beaux toss'd in a Blanket. *page* 2. *line* 41. &c.

(*l*) The Careless Husband, *page* 14. *line* 3. The Female Witt, *page* 31. *line* 11, 14. *p.* 39. *l.* 24, 25. The Portsmouth Heiress, *page* 11. *line* 32. *p.* 55. *l.* 5. *p.* 66. *l.* 13. The Stage Beaux toss'd in a Blanket, *page* 59. *line* 8. *Ah Gad!* The Lawyers Fortune, *page* 64. *line* 13. *Before Gad.* The Confederacy, *page* 17. *line* 13. *By Gad.* The Female-Wits, *page* 33. *line* 18. *Eh Ged!* (affectedly and ridiculously) The Stage Beaux toss'd in a Blanket, *page* 4. *line* 33, 41. *p.* 12. *l.* 16, 32. *p.* 14. *l.* 1. *p.* 43. *l.* penult. *p.* 44. *l.* 26. *p.* 51. *l.* 1, 16. *p.* 52. *l.* 12. *p.* 54. *l.* 14. *p.* 56. *l.* 9. *p.* 58. *l.* 19. *p.* 59. *l.* 5. *Gad forgive me.* The Confederacy, *page* 7. *line* 9. *p.* 46. *l.* 28. The Female Wits, *page* 34. *line* 8. The Stage Beaux toss'd in a Blanket, *page* 51. *line* 20. *O Gad.* The Female Wits, *page* 22 *line* 8. *p.* 32. *l.* 9. *p.* 50. *l.* 24.

(*m*) The Careless Husband, *page* 26. *line* 25. *p.* 50. *l. ult. p.* 51. *l.* 8. *p.* 56. *l.* 31. The The Confederacy, *page* 7. *line* 25. *p.* 24. *l.* 36. *p.* 65. *l.* 18. The Roving Husband reclaim'd, *page* 18. *line* 14. *Eh Lard!* (ridiculously) The Stage Beaux toss'd in a Blanket, *page* 13. *line* 22. *Good Lard!* The Confederacy, *page* 13. *line* 4. *O Lard!* The Confederacy, *page* 13. *line* 7. The Roving Husband recaim'd, *page* 26. *line* 22. The Stage Beaux toss'd in a Blanket, *page* 45. *line* 19. *Oh Lerd!* The Stage Beaux toss'd in a Blanket, *page* 13. *line* 22.

(*n*) Lord Foppington's *Discourse* in The Relapse, *printed* 1698, *and also in* The Careless Husband, *page* 20. *line* 1, *p.* 28, *l.* 35, &c.

which

which the *Players* use, when they
would have any Person or Saying appear contemptible. When they use the
Name of *God*, they speak in such a
Manner as to make it the Jest of the
Play-House; but when they speak of
the *Devil*, they speak with such an
Emphasis as may command Respect and
Attention: And thus whilst they falsly
pretend, that they have avoided one
Sin, they run into another, which hath
a plainer Tendency to *Atheism*, and
strikes more directly at the supream
Authority. As Fops, or Fools speak
on other Occasions, so the *Players* always speak when they mention *The
Great Creator of Heav'n and Earth*.
Such Familiarity with his Transcendent
Majesty, and at such a Time is too apt
to breed a Contempt. The best which
can be made of it, is a (*o*) Jesting or
Trifling with *Holy Things*, which was
always reckon'd an unsafe, if not a vicious Practice. The Word *Heaven* is
sometimes (*p*) us'd for *God* himself,
whose Throne and chief Residence is
there. Accordingly our *Blessed Saviour* tells us (*q*) *Whosoever sweareth by
heaven, sweareth by the throne of God,
and him that sitteth thereon*. For this
                                                    Reason

(*o*) *Non tu-
tum est lude-
re cum sacris.*

(*p*) *Dan. 4.
26. Luke 15.
21.*

(*q*) *Matth.
23. 22.*

Reason I think it not fit to use the
Word upon the *Stage* in (r) this Sense,
and in trifling Matters, or that (s) an
Actor should desire, for *Heavens sake,*
that Care may be taken for the Comit-
ting Adultery in private. This is, in
short, a Representing of *God* as de-
lighting in Iniquity, and Men as wal-
lowing in *Uncleanness* under Pretence
of *Religion*; and if our *Blessed Savi-*
our may be believ'd in the Case of *Oaths,*
the present (t) *Actors* are scandalously
guilty; since *Swearing by Heaven* is
their common *Method.*

(r) *Solon,*
page 66. line
34. p. 68. l. 6.
The Cares of
Love, *page 34.*
line penult. p.
41. *l* 10. The
Female Wits,
page 20. line
8. *p. 22. l. 16.*
p. 27. l. 25. p.
29 *l. 4. p. 50.*
l. penult. p. 57.
l. 18. The
Portsmouth
Heiress, *page*
57. *line* 1.

(s) The
Confederacy,
page 28. line
33.

(t) Liberty Asserted, *page 66, line 30.* Love at first Sight, *page*
15. *line 41. p. 55. Act 4. l. 24. p. 60. l. antepenult. p. 63. l. 28.* Solon, *page 54. line 15. p. 62. l. 27.* The Cares of Love, *page 17. line*
20. *p. 19. l. 14. p. 20. l. 13. p. 23. l. 31. p. 26. l. 34.* The Conquest of Spain, *page 3. line 5. p. 14. l. 11. p. 15. l. 27. p. 22. l. 33. p.*
26. *l. 32. p. 44. l. 15. p. 51. l. 31. p. 55. l. 4. p. 58. l. 5.* The
Faithful Bride of Granada, *page 2. line 19.* The Faithful General, *page*
28. *line. 44.* The Female Wits, *page 2. line 15. p. 4. l. 19. p. 9.*
l. 16. p. 25. l. 5. p. 32. l. 3. p. 45. l. 3. p. 52. l. 17. p. 55. l. ult.
The Loyal Subject, *page 66. line 29, 35.* The Mistake, *page 41, line*
8. The Portsmouth Heiress, *page 28. line 20. p. 49. l. antepenult.* The
Rival Brothers, *page 84. line 5.* The Roving Husband reclaim'd, *page*
61. *line 10. p. 62. l. 18. p. 63. l. 15.* The Royal Merchant, *page*
44. *line 38. p. 48. l. 21. p. 59. l. 18.*

But if this was the only Practice of
the present *Stage*, it might perhaps be
something more tolerable. Alas! They
take a far greater Liberty, and scruple

[*] The Nor-
thern Lass,
page 24. *line*
10.
[*x*] The Roy-
al Merchant,
page 6, *line* 14.
[*y*] The Con-
queſt of Spain
page 52. *line* 2.
The Rival
Brothers, *page*
91. *line* ult.
[*z*] The Con-
queſt of Spain
page 52. *line*
26.
[*] Liberty
Aſſerted, *page*
25. *line* 20.
(‖) The
Faithful Bride
of Granada,
page 29. *line*
18.
(*a*) The Me-
tamorphoſis,
page 151. *line*
5.
(*b*) the Biter,
page 14, *line*
5. *p.* 16. *l.* 22.
p. 23, *l.* 19.

no *Oath* whatſoever. Sometimes they
[*x*] make a Jeſt of our ſolemn Manner
in adminiſtring an *Oath*, by charging
the Perſon *ſworn to ſpeak the Truth, the
whole Truth, and nothing but the Truth,*
as God *ſhall help him.* And as the *ſeri-
ous* Part is turn'd into Ridicule; ſo *profane Oaths* are to be found in every
Play, and (I had almoſt ſaid) in every
Page. Sometimes they ſwear in Words
at Length, [*x*] *By all that's Sacred,* and
[*y*] *By all that's Good,* [*z*] *By the Eternal Truth,* or [*] *Mind,* (‖) *By Heav'n
and Earth, and all that's Dear and Good.*
(*a*) *By all the Powers that hear Oaths,
and rain down Vengeance upon broken
Faith;* (*b*) *By the ſolemn Powers,* and
(*c*) *As they hope to be ſav'd.* Sometimes they *ſwear* both (*d*) *By God* and
a *Woman* preſent upon the *Stage,* as if
they ador'd both alike, or rather look'd
upon a Woman to be the only Good,
and plac'd her above *God* himſelf.

(*c*) Squire Trelooby, *page* 11. *line* 11. The Roving Husband reclaim'd. *page* 11. *line* 9.

(*d*) *By all that's good, By thy bright ſelf I ſwear.* The Conqueſt
of Spain, *page* 52. *line* 2. *By the Gods, By thee thy ſelf the greateſt
Oath to Love.* The Faithful General, *page* 71. *line* 36.

It would puzzle any one at firſt View,
to give a Reaſon why the *Actors* cry out
                                                    O

(e) O *Jehu* in their *Comedies*, since *Jehu* was a furious Man, and a Worshipper of the *Golden Calves*; but the Mystery is at an End when we consider, that it bears the greatest Resemblance to the sacred Name *Jehovah*, of any Word we find in Scripture, and therefore they think it the fittest to become the Jest of the *Play-House*.

Our *Blessed Saviour* cautions us (f) that we should not *swear by Jerusalem, because it is the city of the great king.* For this Reason, I suppose, they swear (p) *by Jericho*, it being a Word like the other in sound, and consequently reflecting on that Command, as much as they dare publickly to be guilty of it.

Our *Blessed Saviour* also cautions us, that (h) we should not *swear by our head, because we cannot make one hair white or black.* How then can they excuse the *profane Language* of the *Play-House* where they commonly *swear*, by their (i) *Blood*, by their (k) *Consci-*

(e) The Female Wits, page 50. line antepenult. p. 52. l. 9.

(f) *Matth.* 5. 35.
(g) The Biter, page 5. line 26. p. 11. l. 4. p. 22. l. 27. p. 24. l. 6.

(h) *Matth.* 5. 36.
(i) Love the Leveller, page 31. line 20.
(k) Gibraltar, page 2. line 11. p. 15. l. 14. Squire Treloby, page 39.

line 16. p. 55. l. 2. The Basset Table, page 6. line 2. p. 19. l. 4. p. 46. l. penult. The Careless Husband, page 13. line 7. p. 38. l. 33. The Confederacy, page 8. line 26. p. 28. l. 34. p. 35. l. 36. p. 71. l. 9. The Fair Example, page 4. line 32. p. 20. l. 30. p. 21. l. 12. p. 33. l. 19 and 21. The Female Wits, page 64. line 11. The Gamester, page 7. line 22. p. 54. l. 20. p. 67. l. penult. The Loyal Subject, page 14. line 36. p. 31. l. 40. p. 43. l. 5. p. 61. l. 12. The Lying Lover, page 62. line 9. The Mistake, page 6. line 27. p. 37 l. 26. The Northern Lass, page 18. line 34. p. 55. l. 20. p. 59. l. 18.

D   ences,

(*l*) Love *ences*; by their (*l*) *Lives*, by their (*m*)
the Leveller, *Souls*, or (*n*) *Bodies?*
page 1. line
11. p. 8. l. 6. p. 21. Act 3. l. 5. p. 23. l. 20. p. 41. l. 24. The
Basset Table, *page* 14. *line* 22. The Loyal Subject, *page* 27. *line* 16.
p. 29. l. 18. p. 42. l. penult. p. 58. l. 20. The Northern Lass, *page*
24. *line* 33. The Portsmouth Heiress, *page* 27. *line* 9. Ulysses,
page 2. line 23.

(*m*) Love at first Sight, *page* 58. *line* 4 *and* 29. own'd to be an Oath
l. 5. Perolla, and Izadora, *page*. 51. *line* 19. Solon, *page* 16. line
25. The Careless Husband, *page* 5. *line* 33. p. 6. l. 40. p. 7. l. 3.
p. 11. l. 14. p. 43. l. 25. p. 45. l. 10. The Female Wits, *page* 66
line 1. The Gamester, *page* 21. *line* 21. The Northern Lass, *page*
58. *line* 7. The Roving Husband Reclaim'd, *page* 59. *line* 20.
The Royal Merchant, *page* 58. *line* 12. The Stage Coach, *page* 4.
line 9. p. 5. l. 5, 25 and 28. p. 6. l. 1. p. 35. l. 1.

(*n*) The Metamorphosis, *page* 21. *line* 8.

But that the Reader may have a
clearer Notion of their most *horrid
Language*, it will be convenient to remember, that in most *Speeches* there
are certain *Rhetorical Figures*, viz. *Aphæ
resis*, when some Letters, or Syllables
are taken away from the Beginning of
a Word; *Paragoge* when they are added to the End of a Word; *Apocope*
when they are taken from the End of
a Word; *Ellipsis*, when some Words
are left out; and *Metathesis*, when
one Letter is plac'd instead of another. No one can be ignorant of this
who hath read the *Latin* and *Greek
Grammars.* Such *Figures* as these are
also used in our *English Dialect.* When
there-

therefore we meet with such Words as in Proper Speech can signify nothing, we are forc'd to reduce them by some of these *Figures*, and then we shall know what the *Authors* aim at. To suppose our *Poets* (those great Masters of *Language*, *Wit* and *Eloquence*) should write *Nonsence*, is a Reflection upon them which they scorn. To suppose them ignorant of these *Figures* in *Rhetorick* is an undervaluing of their Learning: And therefore we must suppose them to be knowingly guilty, and take their Meaning, according as they sometimes explain themselves in other Places. The *Poets* mistrust that such *Hellish Language* in Words at length would not so well go down: And therefore, as *Traitors* formerly clip'd their counterfeit, as well as the real Coin; so do they clip their native *Language*, that the corrupt Part may pass insensibly, and do the greater Mischief. Under this Refuge they think themselves secure, altho' their Pretence is no more to the purpose, than if a *Roman Catholick* should affirm, that he exactly kept *Lent*, because the Meat was minc'd before he swallow'd it. If the bare Letters, and not the Sence did make an

Oath

(o) The StageCoach, page 7. line penult. p. 14. l. antepenult.

(p) An Act at Oxford, page 18. line 14. p. 29. l. 13. p. 34. Act 4. l. 15. Hampstead Heath, page 20. l. 23. p. 32. l. antepenult. p. 39. l. 16. Love at first Sight, page 6. line 3. p. 12. l. 18. p. 14. l. 23. p. 16. l. 22, and 28. p. 23.

Oath, then no Man could *swear*, except in one particular *Language*: Or if putting the Word *Lard* instead of *Lord* can alter the Nature of the Sin; they who live in the *North* of *England* can never be guilty, since it is their common Way of Speaking. So that notwithstanding their frivolous Pretences, and subtle Evasions, wherewith they endeavour to excuse their Crimes, and gild over the Poison, the present *Actors* are horridly guilty of *Swearing* in a most scandalous Manner, beyond the Examples of former Ages; since all these Expressions, *viz.* (o) E-Cod, (p) E-gad, (q) 'Gad, (r) God, (s) I--Cod,

l. 20. p. 50. l. 4. p. 53. l. penult. p. 55. Act 5, l. 6. p. 59. l. 4, and 13. p. 60. l. 32. p. 61. l. 8. p. 62, l. 6. p. 63. l. 2. p. 64. l. 3, 7. 13 and 22. p. 65. l. penult. p. 67. l. antepenult. Squire Trelooby, page 52. line 1. The Basset Table, page 40. line 12. p. 43. l. 7. p. 58. l. 4, 22 and 32. The Biter, page 15, line 19. The Female Wits, page 58, line 12. The Gamester, page 52, line 12. The Lawyers Fortune, page 38. line 7 and 12. The Roving Husband Reclaim'd, page 10. line 20 p. 53. l. ult. p. 56. l. 25. p. 64. l. 9. The Stage Coach, page 2. line 6.

(q) Fortune in her Wits, page 12. line 1. p. 41. l. 22. Gibraltar, page 5. line 33. p. 20 l. 8. p. 22 l. 21 and 24. Sheet H. p. 53. l. 3. p. 57. l. 12. p. 59. l. penult. p. 64. l. ult. Epilogue the Second, l, 19. The Cares of Love, page 37. line 15. p. 48. l. 13. The Female Wits, page 3. line 21. The Roving Husband Reclaim'd, page 55. line 24. p. 65. l. 1.

(r) Squire Trelooby, page 49. line 25.

(s) Hampsfield Heath, page 52. line 13. The Fair Example, page 32. line 2. The Mistake, page 55. line 26. p. 58. l. 15. The Roving Husband Reclaim'd, page 14. line 16. The Stage Coach, page 26. line 10.

[t] I--Gad,

[t] *I--Gad,* (u) *'Od,* and [x] *Y--God,* are positive *Oaths, by God himself,* as they are used in the *Play-House,* by all sorts of Persons, and on all Occasions.

(t) Gibraltar, *page* 43. *line ult. p.* 39. *l.* 5. *Love the Leveller, page* 54. *line* 6.

The Fair Example, *page* 37. *line* 3. The Female Wits, *page* 36. *line* 27. The Mistake, *page* 27. *line* 18. *p.* 28. *l.* 10. *p.* 35. *l.* 1. *p.* 53, *l.* 13.

(u) The Biter, *page* 16. *line* 25, 33 *and* 24. *p.* 17. *l.* 7. *p.* 21. *l.* 19. *p.* 23, *l.* 16. *p,* 25. *l.* 21. *p.* 53. *l.* 33.

(x) The Amorous Miser, *page* 39. *line* 12.

And as they deal thus with the *Name of God;* so they make as bold with *Christ Jesus, our blessed Saviour and Redeemer.* In this Respect they may be said (y) *to crucify to themselves the son of God afresh, and put him to open shame.* These are the Men who by their Words declare, that [z] *they esteem the blood of the covenant wherewith they are sanctified, as a profane thing,* whilst they thus *do despight unto the spirit of grace.* What other meaning can be put upon their frequent and horrid Oaths, by the [†] *Body,* by the (a) *Blood,* by the (b) *Death,* (c) *the Life,* (d) *the Heart,* and (e) *Wounds of God?*

(y) *Heb.* 6. 6.

(z) *Heb.* 10 29.

(†) *Od's Bodykins.* As you had it, printed 1703, *page* 16. *line antepenult. Bodykins.* Love at first Sight, *page* 25. *line* 30. *p.* 26. *l.* 16, *and* 4c. (a) *God's bud.* Gibraltar, *Sheet* F *page* 44, *line* 9. *'D's blood.* An Act at Oxford, *page* 10. *line* 12. *'S blood.* Squire Treiooby, *page* 52. *line* 18.

21. *line* 22. *'Ad's bud.* The Basset Table, *page* 52. *line* 18. *'Ud's bud.* The Lawyers Fortune, *page* 8. *line* 25. *'S bud or 'Z bud.* Gibraltar, *Sheet* F *page* 44. *line* 34. Love the Leveller, *page*

56. line penult. The Amorous Miſer, *page* 1. *line* 9 *and* 12. *p.* 2. *l.* 11, 25 and 32. p. 3. *l.* 16. p. 4. *l.* 4, 13 and 24. *p.* 5. *l.* 27. *p.* 6. *l.* 22. p. 7. *l.* 24. p. 9. *l.* 15 and 22. p. 10 *l.* 20 and 24. *p.* 33. *l.* 10, 22, 25 and 27. p. 34, *l.* 23 *and* 29. p. 35. *l.* 12. *p.* 36. *l.* 22. p. 37. *l.* 1. p. 38. *l.* 23 and 25. *p.* 39. *l.* 16. p. 40. *l.* 28. p. 42. *l.* 15 *and* 17. *p.* 43. *l.* 16. p. 45. *l.* antepenult. p. 47. *l.* 6. *p.* 49. *l.* 16, 27 *twice*, *and l.* 29. *p.* 50. *l.* 7. *p.* 51. *l.* 8. *p.* 52. *l.* 2 and 30. *p.* 53. *l.* 15. *p.* 58. *l.* 12 and 19. *p.* 59. *l.* 10 *and* 22. Forty ſeven times in this one *Comedy.* The Fair Example, *page* 32. *line* 3. *p.* 34. *l.* 5. *p.* 38. *l.* 10.

(*h*) 'Ud's Death. The Miſtake, *page* 48. *line* 19.   'D's Death. Hampſtead Heath, *page* 18. *line* 26. The Baſſet Table, *page* 10. *line* 12.   's Death. Love at firſt Sight, *Epilogue, line* 5. *page* 39. *line* 7. *p.* 43. *l.* 21 and 32. *p.* 47. *l.* 1 *and* antepenult. *p.* 50. *l.* 15. *p.* 56. *l.* pennlt. *p.* 63. *l.* 21. 30 and ult. *p.* 65. *l.* 24. *p.* 67. *l.* 22. Love the Leveller, *page* 22. *line* 12. Solon, *page* 49. *line* 12. *p.* 67. *l.* 19. The Amorous Miſer, *page* 13. *line* 19. *p.* 14. *l.* 23. The Biter, *page* 4. *line* 4. The Cares of Love, *page* 43. *line* 25. *p.* 48. *l.* 27. The Confederacy, *page* 14. *line* 9. *p.* 33. *l.* 3. The Law-yers Fortune, *page* 8. *line* 20. The Portſmouth Neireſs, *page* 31. *line* 4. *p.* 47. *l.* 10 and 28. *p.* 52. *l.* 1. *p.* 54. *l.* 12. The Temple of Love, *Epilogue, line* 3.   Death! Gibraltar, *Sheet* E *page* 33. *line* 20. *Sheet* F *p.* 45. *l.* 26. *p.* 52. *line* 14. *p.* 54. *l.* 35. *p.* 55. *l.* 17 *and* penult. *p.* 60. *l.* 27. Love at firſt Sight, *page* 57. *line* 30. The Amorous Miſer, *page* 11. *line* 3. The Baſſet Table, *page* 39. *line* 31. The Careleſs Husband, *page* 4. *line* 1. *p.* 6. *l.* 10. *p.* 17. *l.* 37. *p.* 18. *l.* 39. *p.* 28. *l.* 12 and 41. *p.* 47. *l.* ult. *p.* 55. *l.* 7. *p.* 62. *l.* 30. *p.* 64. *l.* 3. The Conqueſt of Spain, *page* 60. *line* 26. The Gameſter, *page* 4. *line* 21. *p.* 45. *l.* 32. *p.* 55. *l.* 14. The Quacks, *page* 83, *line* 21. The Roving Husband reclaim'd, *page* 39, *line* 22.

(*c*) 'Od's Life. Loves Contrivance, (*printed* 1703) *page* 23, *line* 5. *p* 60, *l* 29.   'Ud's Life. The Miſtake, *page* 3, *line* ult.   's Life. Gibraltar, *Sheet* F *page* 44, *line* 18. p 56, *l* 17. The Amorous Miſer, *page* 39, *line* 1. The Portſmouth Heireſs, *page* 36, *line* 13. p 63, *l* 7, 11 and 13.   'Life. Gibraltar, *Sheet* F *page* 43. *line* 1.

(*d*)'s Heart. Love at firſt Sight, *page* 25, *line* 17. p 28, *l* 24. 30 and 36. p 30, *l* 9. p 38, *l* 9. p 41, *l* 3 and 31. p 42, *l* 4, 10 *and* penult. p 47, *l* 5, 9 and 32. p 48, *l* 7 *and* 22. p 52, *l* 1 and 14. p 53, *l* 24 and 31. p 54, *l* 18, 21 *and* penult. p 60, *l* 17, 21 *and* 26. p 61, *l* 3. p 62, *l* 12. p 63, *l* 3, 9, 12 *and* 37. p 64, *l* 11 *and* 18. p 65, *l* 9 and 29. p 67, *l* 3, 7, 16, 25 *and* 32.
                                                                    'Ad's Heart.

However, whilst the *Actors* take this Method to avoid the Penalty of the Law, and yet retain the *Sins* against *God,* in Despight of all the Attempts for their *Reformation* ; and whilst they thus profanely *swear, by the death of Christ,* and *his Blood,* which was shed for the Redemption of fallen Man, it might be expected, that they would join it with some Expressions of Respect and Esteem : But instead thereof they join it with Words of Contempt and Reproach, as if they look'd upon that stupendous Miracle of Mercy, to be the greatest Calamity that could befall the World. What other Meaning can there be of such Expressions as these? [f] *Blood and Death, and Fire!* [g] *Blood and Thunder!* [h]*'s Death and Amazement!*

[f] The Gamester, *page* 52, *line* 14.
[g] The Confederacy, *page* 13, *line* 8. p 67, l 22. p 50. l 30, *owned to be an Oath ibid.* l 31. The Fair Example, *page* 34. *line* 18.
[h] The Portsmouth Heiress, *page* 38, *line* 1.

D 4   [i] *Death*

[*i*] The [*i*] *Death and Confusion!* [*k*] *Death and*
Fair Example, *Destruction!* [*l*] *Torture and Death!*
page 42, line
18. p 59. l 31. and that which is yet more monstrously
The Mistake, impious, [*m*] *'D's Death and Furies!*
page 58, line 1.
[*k*] The [*n*] *Death and Furies!* [*o*] *Death and*
Roving Huf- *Hell!* [*p*] *Death, Hell and Furies!* [*q*]
band Re-
claim'd, page *Death and the Devil!*
41 line 7.

[*l*] The Portsmouth Heiress, *page* 45, *line* 26.

[*m*] An Act at Oxford, *page* 36, *line penult.*

[*n*] The Confederacy, *page* 13, *line* 15. p 45, l 7. p 33, l 7. *owned
to be an Oath ibid.* l 8.

[*o*] Gibraltar, *page* 54, *line* 27.

[*p*] The British Enchanters, *page* 29, *Act* 4, *line* 4. The Faithful General, *page* 53, *line* 7.

[*q*] Gibraltar, *page* 49, *line* 9. p 58, l 29. The Confederacy,
page 29, *line ult.* P 50. l 25, *owned to be an Oath, ibid.* L 26.

The bare Repetition of such unparal-
lel'd *Blasphemy*, will make the Flesh
tremble, and the Blood grow cold.
A just Reflection hereon cannot be express'd in Words, and therefore I must
leave the Reader, to make it himself,
and then to apply the Expostulation of
(*r*) 2 *Cor.* St. *Paul*, (*r*) *What concord hath Christ
6. 15, 17. with Belial? Wherefore come ye out from
among them, and be ye separate, saith
the Lord, and touch not the unclean
thing; and I will receive you.*

To these *Horrid Oaths*, may several
Instances be added from our present
Plays, besides those already mentioned in
The

The British Enchanters, where (s) the *Devils* appear on the *Stage,* and (t) are oftentimes made a Jest for the *Hearers,* as if they believed no such thing in earnest, and sometimes the *Adoration* due to *God* alone is paid to them. This is certainly the highest *Blasphemy* that Mortals can invent, 'tis enough to make the Hair stand upright, and it might be thought that none but *Persons* given over to a *Reprobate Sense* can take Pleasure in such Diversions.

(s) Solon, *page* 30, *line* antepenult. The Roving Husband Reclaim'd, *page* 58, *line* 20.

(t) Fortune in her Wits, *page* 27, *line* 31. Gibraltar, *Sheet* F *page* 44, *line* 30 *and* 36. The Roving Husband Reclaim'd, *page* 8, *line* 21.

The Devil a Wit (i. e. *No Wit*) The Northern Lass, *Prologue, line* 5. *The Devil a one* (i. e. *No one*) The Portsmouth Heiress, *page* 54, *line* 4. *The Devil a Thing* (i. e. *Not any Thing*) The Stage Coach, *page* 32, *line* 3.

I cannot but observe that these Representations (tho' the Diversion of the *English Stage*) were accounted scandalous in foreign Countries, and accordingly the Use of Vizards representing *Devils* were prohibited by *Canons* made for this Purpose, (u) one threatning *Excommunication* for the Offence, and (x) another telling us that this Practice

(u) Synodus Lingonensis, An. 1404. Summopere caveant ne interfint, neque ludant in Ludo, quo utuntur Larvis in figurâ Dæmonum, & horrenda ibidem committuntur: quem Ludum, prohibemus sub non solùm Clericis, sed generaliter omnibus subditis Excommunicationis pænâ, & decem Librarum nobis applicandarum.

(x) Concilium Nanatense, Anno 890. Nullus Presbyterorum Larvas Dæmonum ante se fieri consentiat: quia hoc Diabolicum est, & sacris Canonibus prohibitum.

is

is *Diabolical, and forbidden in the Holy Scriptures* ; but in our new *Theatre*, there are such things publickly acted, which those who lived under *Popish Superstition*, and in the grossest Times of Ignorance were asham'd of, and judg'd to be utterly unlawful.

But to instance in Particulars.

First, To (b) own the *Devil* as a *God*, or make a Compact with him for the gratifying of our Revenge, is *a Sin* so positively forbidden in the *first Commandment*, and (c) other *Texts* of *Scripture*, as will admit of no Evasions. To call him a *more than mortal Power*, and infer from thence, that it is a *Frenzy* to resist him and his Agents, is also as dreadful : and yet this is the *Blasphemous Language* of the *Stage*, and such a Comment upon *St. James* as is not to be met with, except in the *Play-House* lately built for *Reformation*.

Secondly, We are commanded in weighty Matters, and for the Deciding of Controversies, to (f) *swear by the Name of God, in truth, in judgment, and in righteousness*. This is a solemn Calling of him to be a Witness of what we say ; it is an Acknowledg-
ment

(b) The British Enchanters, *page* 12, *line* 22.

(c) 1 *Sam.* 28. 7, 11, *compared with* 1 *Chron.* 10. 13, 14.

(d) The British Enchanters, *page* 16, *line* 2.

(e) *James* 4. 7.

(f) *Deut.* 10. 20. *Jer.* 4. 2. *Hebrews* 6. 16.

ment that he ſearcheth the Hearts, and will render Vengence on that Man, who *ſwears falſely*, and conſequently is an Act of Worſhip due to *God* alone ; but this in the *Play-Houſe* is paid to the *Devil.* Thus (*g*) in the *Play* call'd *Solon*, the Scene is *Hell*, and *Pluto* ſwears at large,

(*g*) *Page* 30, *l.* 10.

By the Horrors of the Deep,
By Chaos, *Darkneſs*, Night *and* Sleep,
By all the Torments here below,
By all the fiery Streams that flow.

Thus they frequently *ſwear*, by (*h*) *Hell*, by (*i*) *the Furies*, and (*k*) *the Devil*; as if that was true of them, which the *Prophet Iſaiah* ſpeaks. (*l*) *We have made a covenant with death, and with hell we are at agreement, for we have made lies our refuge, and under falſhood have we hid our ſelves.*

(*b*) The Gameſter, *page* 45, *line ult.* The Lawyers Fortune, *page* 30, *line* 1. Zelmane, *page* 34, *line* 14.

(*i*) The Faithful Bride of Granada, *page* 43, *line* 3. The Gameſter, *page* 55, *line* 4. p 56, l 1.
(*k*) An Act at Oxford, *page* 26, *line* 16. The Gameſter, *page* 55, *line* 9.
(*l*) *Iſaiah* 28. 15.

Thirdly, We are commanded in Scripture, to (*m*) *call upon the name of the* Lord

(*m*) *Geneſ.* 12. 8. Pſal. 20. 5. Acts 22. 16.

(*n*) *Acts* Lord, and (*n*) all *Adjurations* are made
3. 6. *and* 16. in the *Name of God*, or of *Christ*; but
18. *and* 19. in the *Play-House* they *adjure, in the*
13. *Name* of the (*o*) *Devil*, (*p*) *Lucifer*
(*o*) Squire and (*q*) *Satan.*
Trelooby,
page 22. *line*
8. p 38, l 23. The Confederacy, *page* 51, *line* 12. The
Fair Example, *page* 3, *line* 1. p 6, l 16. The Stage Coach,
page 31, *line* 7.

(*p*) The Confederacy, *page* 38, *line* 32.

(*q*) The Amorous Miser, *page* 48, *line* 1.

(*r*) Love *Fourthly,* All *Ejaculations* in *Scrip-*
at first Sight, *ture* are spoken in the Name of *God*:
page 15, *line* but in the *Play-House* they are spoken
antepenult. in the Name of the *Devil.* Thus
p 17, l 25. *Psal.* 15. 1. *Lord! who shall abide?*
(*s*) An Act *&c.* but the *Play-House Language* is,
at Oxford, *who the Devil? &c.* Indeed some-
page 18, *line* times they use (*r*) the Name of *God*,
20. p 35, l on such Occasions (tho I wish they
1. Gibral- did not) but generally the *Devil* is
tar, *Sheet* F set in *God's* Place: And as the *Church*
page 41, *line* of *Rome* have Ten *Ave Marias* for One
13. *Sheet* F *Pater Noster*; so the Respect of (*s*)
p 44, l 23. this Kind, which they pay to the *De-*
Sheet F p 46, *vil*, is Ten Times as much as that
l 12. *Sheet* G which they pay to *God. Good Lord,*
p 56, l 22. deliver us from such *Synagogues of*
Sheet H p 49, *Satan,* and from such Men who are
l 5. *Sheet* H thus publickly devoted to his Service.
p 53, l 9. p
62, l 17.
Hampstead
Heath, *page*
39, *line* 120.
Love at first
Sight, *page* 48, *line* 21, Love the Leveller, *page* 6, *line* 18.
　　　　　　　　　　　　　　　　　　Squire

Squire Trelooby, *page* 21, *line* 5. p 35, l 28. The Amorous Miſer, *page* 51, *line* 7. The Baſſet Table, *page* 2, *line* 8 *and* 15. p. 21, l 1, 23 *and* 33. p 31, l 15 *and antepenult.* p 40, l 2. The Biter, *page* 1, *line* 11. p 2, l 29. p 52, l 5. The Britiſh Enchanters, *page* 12, *line* 1. The Careleſs Husband, *page* 19, *line* 36. p 23, l 22. The Cares of Love, *page* 37, *line* 7. p 39, l 4. p 47, l 5. p 48, l 30. The Confederacy, *page* 17, *line* 11. p 22, l 26. p 31, Act 3, l 1. The Fair Example, *page* 63, *line* 9. The Female Wits, *page* 22, *line* 18. p 29, l. 10. p 63, l 16. p 64, l *penult.* The Gameſter, *page* 1, *line* 1. p 4, l 5 *and* 15. p 23, l *antepenult.* p 57, l 14. The Loyal Sub- ject, *page* 21, *line* 17. The Metamorphoſis, *page* 32, *line* 14. p 41, l 19. The Miſtake, *page* 8, *line* 15. p. 28, l 16. p 32, l *ult.* The Northern Laſs, *page* 69, *line* 34. The Roving Husband Reclaim'd, *page* 9, *line* 21. The Stage Coach, *page* 25, *line* 4. p 28, l 14. p 29, l 1. The Tender Husband, *page* 60 *twice, in line* 27 *and* 28. Ulyſſes, *Epilogue, line* 33.

Laſtly, Prayers to, and *Praiſes* of an Inviſible Being as preſent, are Acts of *Divine Worſhip*, and due to *God* a- lone ; and if we believe the *Scriptures*, ought to be given to none other. When the *Devil* tempted our *Saviour* to worſhip him, his Suggeſtions were repell'd by ſaying (*t*) *It is written* (*t*) *Matth.* *thou ſhalt worſhip the Lord thy God and* 4. 10. *him only ſhalt thou ſerve.* The Good *Angel* alſo refus'd the ſame, and gave this Reaſon (*u*) *We muſt worſhip God.* (*x*) *Rev.* But both theſe Acts of Adoration are 22. 9. paid to the *Devil* in the *Play-Houſe.* (*x*) Gibral- They ſometimes droll out the Name tar, *page* 5. of (*x*) *the Lord*, to render it deſpiſe- *line* 1. able, and invoke the Aſſiſtance of (*y*) Gib- his *ſacred Majeſty* in (*y*) a *drunken,* raltar, *ibid.*

or

[z] Gibraltar, page 22, line 19.

[a] Squire Trelooby, page 20, line 1 and antepenault. p 21, l 10. The Lawyers Fortune, page 8, line 29.

[b] The British Enchanters, page 30, line 30.

[c] The British Enchanters, page 16, line 2.

[d] The British Enchanters, page 12, line 22.

[e] *John* 3. 2.

[f] 1 *Cor.* 14, 25.

[g] The Gamester, page 6, line 22.

[h] The Biter, page 3, line 7.

[i] The Basset Table, page 27, line 14. The Biter, page 61, line 16. The Careless Husband, page 17, line 32. p 20. l 17.

(k) *Mat.* 12. 31, 32. *Mark* 3. 22 to 30. *Luk.* 12. 10.

or [z] a *Whoring Intreague*, or upon [a] *ridiculous Occasions*; but they use the grand Rebel against *Heav'n* at another Rate, they [b] pray to him to *aid their just designs*, they own him as [c] *more than a mortal* Power, nay [d] as a *God*, and pronounce his Name with an *Emphasis*, as if it was more remarkable. When any Person is mention'd in *Scripture* as of Extraordinary Abilities, the usual Expression is, that [e] *God is with him*, or [f] *in him*; but in the *Play-House Language* [g] *He is the Devil*, or [h] *the Devil is in him*: And when any Person is over-rul'd by some unexpected *Providence*, presently [i] *the Devil is in it*, and the Glory given to him alone.

When the *Pharisees* attributed our *Saviour's Miracles* to the Power of the Devil, he said that (k) they were guilty of the *Sin against the Holy Ghost*

and

and that this Sin alone *should never be forgiven*: Now how near the ascribing the works of *God's Providence* to the Devil in this Age, comes up to the unpardonable Sin of the *Pharisees*, they who are guilty ought seriously to consider; for it is no jesting Matter.

I am sensible that the Reader may think, I wrong the *Players* in affirming, that in a *Christian Nation*, and before an Assembly of People, such Persons, who in their *Baptismal Vow* have promised *to renounce the Devil and all his works*, shall dare to *pray* or sing *Praises* to him; and therefore I am forc'd to produce some Quotations to this purpose. I shall make no *Comment* on the *Monsters*; but let others judge whether I misrepresent them or not.

Arsinoe, page 22. line 2.

Assist, ye Furies, from the Deep,
Revenge, Revenge prepare.

The British Enchanters, *page* 30. line 30.

Furies, Alecto, aid my just Design.

The

The Metamorphosis, *page* 14.

Hail, Pow'rs beneath, whose Influence
                              [*imparts*
The Knowledge of Infernal Arts ;
By whose unerring Gifts we move
To alter the Decrees above ;
Whether on Earth, or Seas, or Air,
The mighty Miracle we dare.

(*l*) The Monthly Collection of Vocal Musick, for October, 1704.

It is Pity to see so noble a Science, as *Musick* thus debas'd. However, the *Devil* must own himself particularly oblig'd to Mr. *Eccles* for this Signal Service in (*l*) composing the Notes on this Occasion, with an Air so like to a *Supplicatory Anthem.*

[*m*] Love the Leveller, *page* 35.
The Temple of Love, *Act* 1. *Scene* 1.
[*n*] The Temple of Love, *page* 30, *and* 34.
[*o*] The Amorous Miser, *page* 40. *line* 1.
[*p*] Ulysses, *page* 6. *line* 21.

The *Players* treating the *Devil* in such a manner ; the Respects which they pay to *Pagan Deities*, will the less be wonder'd at. Accordingly, here we [*m*] have *Temples* in their Honour, [*n*] *Oracles* given which are fulfill'd, tho' strange and mysterious, and Acts of Divine Worship paid to them. In one [*o*] *Play*, *Bacchus* is own'd as a *God*; in [*p*] another, as the Jolly *God of Pleasures*; and accordingly, he is ador'd and invok'd with crowning the Goblet, and *Pagan* Superstitions. In

one

one (*q*) *Play*, after a Clap of *Thunder*, the *Scene* opens above, and discovers *Pallas* in the Clouds; the *Actors* all kneel, and one after another put up their several Petitions; nay they are exhorted so to do in this Expression,

She shakes her dreadful Ægis from the Clouds,
Bend, bend to Earth, and own the present Deity.

In another (*r*) *Play* is represented a magnificent *Temple*, in the midst, an Image of *Jupiter* in *Gold*, arm'd with *Thunderbolts*, standing upon a large *Pedestal*; an *Altar* flaming with *Sacrifice*, several Persons kneeling before it, the *Priests* waiting round it, crown'd with *Gold*; *Choristers* on each side, in *White*, and in *Rows*, with *soft Musick*, and an *Hymn* beginning with these Words.

O King of Gods! Immortal Jove! To thee
Our grateful Incense, and our Hymns we raise.

In the Primitive Times there were many Thousand *Christians* put to Death,

(*q*) Ulysses, *page* 35, *line* 5.

(*r*) The Faithful General, *Page* 25, *Act* 3.

E   which

which they chose rather than they would offer *Incense* to the *Pagan Gods*; but their Examples are out of Mind, and we commit the *Sin* without any Scruple. Now he who confiders (*s*) the great Care of *God* to forbid the *Jews* every Thing, which had a Tendency to *Idolatry* or *Pagan Superstition*, may wonder to see their *Temples*, their *Priests*, their *Altars* and their *Devotions* thus represented on the *Christian Stage*; and tho', blessed be *God*, there is not the Danger of *Paganism*, yet *Atheism* may be the Consequence thereof. For when Men see these *Idols* worshipped with the same Devotion as is given to the true *God*, they are apt to think that all *Religions* are alike, and that it is not the Excellency of any, but only the Education or Fashion of the Country, which make us differ in these Particulars.

(s) Spencer *de ritualibus* Judæorum, *per totum.*

The *Scriptures* enjoin us for this Reason (*t*) *to make no mention of the Names of other Gods,* neither *to let them be heard out of our mouths* : They forbid us (*u*) *to swear by them, to serve them,* and *to bow our selves down unto them,* because such things will

be

(t) Exod. 23. 13. Deut. 12. 3. Judg. 2. 2. Psal. 16. 4. Isaiah 44. 9 to 21. Hos. 2. 17. Zech. 13. 2.
(u) Jos. 23. 7.

be (*x*) *a snare unto us.* Besides, *God* tells us (*y*) *that he is the Lord, that is his name, and he will not give his glory to another, nor his praise to graven images.* Nay, *Origen* (*z*) assures us, That *the Christians* in his Time *contended even to Death, rather than they would call* Jupiter *a God ; and behaved themselves with that Reverence and Piety towards* God, *that they would not attribute to him any of those Names which the Poets gave to any of their imagined Deities.* But our present *Actors* far outdo the utmost of *Pagan Superstition* in this Particular : Here the *Fates* are represented as [*a*] *appointing our Deaths.* Here the *Pagan Gods* and *Goddesses* are represented as [*b*] *immortal,* as [*c*] *bounteous,* as [*d*] *indulgent,* as [*e*] *just,* nay [*f*] *all just,* as [*g*] *knowing,* and [*h*] *wise,* as [*i*] *cœlestial* Pow'rs, and *Guardians of the Just,* as [*k*] *the greater and lesser Pow'rs that rule in Heav'n and Earth,* as [*l*] *such who hear Pray'rs*

(*x*) Exod. 23. 33. *and* 34. 12. Deut. 7. 16.

(*y*) *Isaiah* 42. 8.

(*z*) *Contra* Celsum, lib. 1.

[*a*] Arsinoe, page 38, line antepenult.

[*b*] Arsinoe, page 47, line 16. Fortune in her Wits, page 22, line 26.

[*c*] Perolla and Izadora, page 47, line 6.

[*d*] Perolla and Izadora, page 26, line 29.

[*e*] The British Enchanters, page 30, line 33.

[*f*] Perolla and Izadora, page 59, line 1.

[*g*] Perolla and Izadora, page 18, line 9.
[*h*] Solon, page 12. line penult.
[*i*] Ulysses, page 63, line 10.
[*k*] Ulysses, page 28, line 24.
[*l*] Solon, page 71, line 33. Zelmane, page 13, line 5.

E 2
and

[m] Solon, page 51, line 26.

[n] Perolla and Izadora, page 28, line 6.

[o] Perolla and Izadora, page 29, line 27.

[p] Arsinoe, page 16, line 12 and 20.

[q] The Roving Husband Reclaim'd, page 29, line 10.

[r] The Cares of Love, page 19, line 18.

[s] Perolla and Izadora, page 27, line 31.

[t] The British Enchanters, page 16, line 31.

[u] The British Enchanters, page 19, line antepenult.

[x] Fortune in her Wits, page 17, line 6.

[y] Ulysses, page 3, line 9.

[z] Solon, page 30, line penult.

and give *Victory*, as [m] *such whose Power is boundless, and Wisdom infinite*, as [n] *such who in pity of our Infirmities afford us providential Means*, and [o] as *Witnesses of our Devotion.* Here we have *Cupid* represented as *a* [p] *God*, as [q] *Almighty*, and [r] *as a powerful God*, who alone hath *conquer'd the Learned and the Brave, and frustrated their Resolutions.* This is the *Actors* Exposition of *Job* 5. 12, 13. They represent (s) *Cupid* as the *God of resistless Fire, who oft in Female Hearts with Triumph sees the unlook'd for Changes of his wanton Power*; as (t) *the Creator of Heav'n and Earth, Delight of Gods above, to whom all Nature ows her Birth*, and (u) *one whom no Pow'r can withstand, but he rules from the Skies to the Center.* They represent *Mars*, as (x) *a Guardian God, to whom we chiefly owe our Preservation.* They represent *Nemesis* as (y) *just, and one who knows the Crimes and Injuries of others*; and *Pluto* as (z) *a great Being, reversing the Sentences passed upon Men.*

They

They represent *Jove* as (*a*) *Almighty*, (*a*) Solon, as (*b*) *an Avenger*, (*c*) as *the Creator* page 12, *line* of *the World*, as (*d*) *Eternal*, (*e*) *Im-* 16. The Faith-*mortal*, (*f*) *Imperial*, and *King of the* page 25, line Gods, (*g*) *in Grandeur above*, (*h*) *Just*, ¹³. (*b*) Ulysses, (*i*) one who knows the Crimes and Inju-page 30, line 3. ries of others, (*k*) Supream, (*l*) the (*c*) The Faithful Gene-*Thunderer*, (*m*) *Vindictive*, and (*n*) one ral, page 25, who scourgeth the Flagicious World, and line 12. *then forgives.* (*d*) The Faithful Ge-neral, *ibid.*

(*e*) Perolla and Izadora, *page* 46, *line* 33. The Faithful General, *page* 25, *Act* 3, *line* 1.
(*f*) The British Enchanters, *page* 30, *line* 30. The Faithful Ge-neral, *page* 25, *Act* 3. *line* 1.
(*g*) Arsinoe, page 48, line 1.
(*b*) Ulysses, page 3, line 9.
(*i*) Ulysses, *ibid.*
(*k*) The Faithful General, page 25, line 12.
(*l*) Ulysses, page 34, line 35. The Faithful General, page 26, line 13.
(*m*) Ulysses, *ibid.*
(*n*) Fortune in her Wits, page 19, line 15.

To set this Matter in a clearer Light, it will be requisite to produce some of the *Play-House Language,* and com-pare it with *Scripture* Expressions; and accordingly I shall only take three Passages out of the *Tragedy* of *Ulysses.*

The *Scripture* speaks (*o*) thus of *Christ.* (*o*) *Prov.* 9. 23, *to* 32.
I was set up from everlasting, from the beginning, or ever the earth was.

When

*When there were no depths I was brought
forth, when there were no fountains a-
bounding with water.   When he gave to
the sea his decree, that the waters should
not pass his commandment, when he appointed the foundations of the earth.
Then I was by him as one brought up
with him; I was daily his delight, re-
joycing always before him.*

The P*lay-House* expresseth it thus.

(p) Ulysses, page 42, line 1

(p) So Jove *look'd down upon the War of
   Atoms*
And rude tumultuous Chaos, *when as yet
Fair Nature, Form and Order had no
   Being,
But Discord and Confusion ruin'd all.
Calm and serene upon his Throne he sate,
Fix'd there by the eternal Law of Fate,
Safe in himself because he knew his Power,
And knowing what he was, he knew him-
   self secure.*

(q) Acts 4. 27, 28.

The *Scriptures* speak (q) thus of G*od's*
Over-ruling P*rovidence.*

*Herod and Pontius Pilate, with the
gentiles and people of Israel were gather-
ed together.   For to do whatsoever the
                                           hand*

hand and the counsel of God had determined before to be done.

The Play-House (r) expresseth it thus. (r) Ulysses, page 59, line 9.

——*'Tis certainly decreed,*
Fix'd as the Law by which Imperial Jove
According to his Prescience and his Power,
Ordains the Sons of Men to good or evil.

The Scripture speaks (s) thus of God's Protection in Dangers. (s) Psal. 139. 8, 9, 10.

If I ascend up into heaven, thou art there: if I make my bed in hell, behold thou art there. If I take the wings of the morning, and dwell in the uttermost parts of the sea: even there shall thy hand lead me, and thy right hand shall hold me.

The Stage (t) expresseth it thus. (t) Ulysses, page 61, line 1.

In stormy Seas, in those dread Regions where
Swarthy Cimmerians *have their dark Abode,*
Divided on this World, and borderers on Hell,
Ev'n there the Providence of Jove *was with me,*

De-

Defended, chear'd, and bore me through
the Danger.

It is alfo obfervable that in the worft
Times of *Paganifm*, when they made
Fortune a Goddefs ; *Juvenal*, an Hea-
then, complains of it. *(u)*

(*u*) Satyra
10 *verfe ult.*

Nullum Numen abeft, fi fit Prudentia,
fed te
Nos facimus Fortuna Deam, cæloque lo-
camus.

(*x*) The
Britifh En-
chauters, page
28, line *penult.*
and p 29, l 9.

And yet *Chriftians* are now funk into
thefe very Dregs, as appears from (*x*)
thefe Lines in a late *Comedy.*

To Fortune give immortal Praife,
Fortune depofes and can raife.
All is as Fortune fhall beftow,
'Tis Fortune governs all below.

There are three Acts of Worfhip due
to *God* alone, which in the *Play-Houfe*
are frequently paid to *Pagan Deities.*

(*y*) Arfinoe,
page 2, line 1,
penult. p 3, l

Firft, *Prayer* to them. Sometimes they
pray (*y*) to the Gods in general, and

15, 18. p 9, l 8. p 12, l 3, 15. p 13, l 10. p 18, l 17. p 19, l 16. p 25,
l 1. p 33, l 4, 22. p 40, l 8. p 43, l 17. p 47, l 16.   Fortune in her
Wits, page 22, line 26.   Perolla and Izadora, page 26, line 29. p 34,
l 12. p 43, l *ult.* p 47, l 6. p 63, l 11.   Solon, page 11, Scene 2,
line 2. p 56, l *ult.* p 65, 18.   The Britifh Enchanters, page 8, line
19. p 30, l 33.   Zelmane, page. 13, line 5.

                                        fometimes

fometimes in particular, to (*z*) *Bac-* (*z*) Ulyffes;
chus, to (*a*) *Cupid*, to (*b*) *Diana*, to page 6, line
(*c*) *Hymen*, to (*d*) *Jove*, to (*e*) the 19.
Moon: and as the *Jews* were blamed (*a*) Arfinoe, page 4, line 4;
in *Scripture* (*f*) for burning *Incenfe* to p 42, l 2.
her, by the Name of the *Queen of Hea-* Izadora, page
ven; fo in the *Play-Houfe* fhe is called 27, line 31.
(*g*) *Queen of Darknefs*, and *Queen of* Lafs, page 72,
Night. They alfo *pray* to (*h*) *Neptune*, line 9. The
to (*i*) *Pallas*, to (*k*) *Pluto*, to (*l*) the Heirefs, page
Stars, and to (*m*) *Venus*. 21, line 12. p
25, l 7. p 28,
l antepennlt. p ult, l 24.

(*b*) Fortune in her Wits, page 26, line 25.
(*c*) The Roving Husband Reclaim'd, page 27, line 15.
(*d*) Perolla and Izadora, page 45, line 30.   Solon, page 70,
line 14.   The Faithful General, page 26, line 12.   Ulyffes, page
28, line 22.
(*e*) Arfinoe, page 1, line 1.
(*f*) Jer. 44. 25, 26, 27.
(*g*) Arfinoe, page 1, line 1.
(*h*) Ulyffes, page 28, line 22.
(*i*) Ulyffes, page 35, line 7.
(*k*) Ulyffes, page 28, line 22.
(*l*) Arfinoe, page 25, line 5.
(*m*) Fortune in her Wits, page 25, line 2.   The Female Wits,
page 52, line ult.   The Portfmouth Heirefs, page 40, line 5.   Ulyffes, page 15, line 14.

Secondly, *Praifing* of them, efpecial- (*n*) Ulyffes,
ly with *Hymns*, giving them *Thanks*, page 63, line 10.
and afcribing to them the *Bleffings* which 49. *and* 27. 29.
Men enjoy.   Thefe *Acts* are performed and 28. 9.
fometimes in general, to (*n*) *the Gods*; Luke 1. 28.
fometimes with (*o*) *Scripture* Expref- John 19. 3.
fions,

(p) The fions, and fometimes in particular to
British En- (p) *Cupid*, to (q) *Jove*, to (r) *Mars*,
chanters, page and (s) the *Stars*.
12. *line* 7.

(q) The
Faithful General, *page* 25. *Act* 3. *line* 1. Solon, *page* 2. *line* 6. p
12. l 16.

(r) Fortune in her Wits, *page* 17. *line* 6.

(s) The Rival Brothers, *page* 18. *line* 22.

(t) Perolla Thirdly, *Swearing* by them. Some-
and Izadora, times they *swear* by (t) the *Gods* in ge-
page 29. *line* neral, fometimes in particular, by (u)
29. Solon, *Cupid*, by (x) *Hercules*, by (y) *Jove*,
page 56. *line* 5.
The British and (z) *Juno*, by (a) *Mars*, by (b)
Enchanters, *Neptune*, by (c) *Pallas*, and by (d) *Ve-*
page 8. *line* 35.
The Faithful *nus*; fometimes by (e) all the *Powers*,
General page, fometimes by (f) the *Stars*, fome-
28. *line* 46. p.
36. l 42. p 68.
l 39. The Female Wits, *page* 44. *line* 9. The Gamefter, *page* 40.
line ult.

(u) Liberty Afferted, *page* 14. *line* 17. Solon, *page* 64. *line* 19.

(x) The Fair Example, *page* 9. *line* 19. The .Gamefter, *page*
56. *line* 11.

(y) Gibraltar, *page* 59. *line* 35. Solon, *page* 40. *line* 28. p 71.
l. 6. The Confederacy, *page* 13. *line penult.* The Female Wits,
page 44. *line* 12. The Gamefter, *page* 31. *line* 11. Ulyffes, *page* 4.
line 29. p 30. l 3. p 41. l 21.

(z) The Gamefter, *page* 52. *line* 12. Ulyffes, *page* 11. *line* 17.
p 12. l 25.

(a) The Amorous Mifer, *page* 45. *line* 3. Ulyfies, *page* 40 *line* 18.

(b) The Baffet Table, *page* 22. *line* 11.

(c) Ulyffes. *page* 41. *line* 21.

(d) The Fair Example, *page* 7. *line antepenult.* The Loyal
Subject, *page* 70. *line* 3. The Northern Lafs, *page* 52. *line* 15.
Ulyffes *page* 3. *line penult.*

(e) Zelmane, *page* 45. *line* 26.

(f) Zelmane, *page* 39. *line* 22.

times

times by (*g*) their *guardian Stars*, and sometimes by the All-seeing *Sun*. To this I shall add, That sometimes they (*i*) intreat *for Jupiter's sake*, and sometimes adjure (*k*) *in the Name of Jove*, and (*l*) *in the Name of Wonder*. Besides, they frequently imitate *Thunder*; a Crime, I think, peculiar to *Caligula* and *Salmoneus*, two of the vilest *Heathens*, and to the *English Stage*: And as the *Scripture* (*m*) reckons this as one of the glorious Works of *God*; so the *Actors* (*n*) sometimes ascribe it to the *Pagan Deities*, but (*o*) generally to the Power of the *Devil*. In the Scripture [*p*] *God* is said to cast forth *Lightnings*; in the *Play-House* [*q*] they are the Effect of *Magical Arts* and *Conjurations*.

(*g*) Zelmane, *page* 4. line 18.

(*h*) Zelmane, *page* 27. line 27.

(*i*) The Confederacy, *page* 22. line 37.

(*k*) The Confederacy, *page* 50. line 35.

(*l*) The Biter, *page* 40. line 23.

(*m*) *Exod.* 9. 23. 1 *Sam.* 2. 10, *and* 7. 10, *and* 12. 17, 18 2 *Sam.* 22. 14. *Job* 26 19, *and* 37 4, 5 *and* 40. 9. *Psalm* 18. 13. *and* 29 3, *and* 77 18.

(*n*) Ulysses, *page* 34. *line* 35. *p.* 35. *l.* 7 *and* 25.

(*o*) The British Enchanters, *page* 1. *Scene* 1. *line* 5. *p.* 39. *L.* 12. See *below in the Reference* [*q*]

[*p*] 2 *Sam.* 22. 15. *Job* 38. 25, 35. *Psal.* 18. 14, *and* 77. 18, *and* 97. 4, *and* 135. 7, *and* 144. 6. *Jer.* 10. 13.

[*q*] Mackbeth, *Printed* 1695, *Act* 1. *Scene* 1. *line* 1, *and* 2. *page* 3. *l.* 21. The British Enchanters, *page* 16, *line* 19. *P.* 33, *l.* penult. *p.* 34, *l.* 8.

And as they *swear* by the *Pagan Deities*; so they frequently *swear* by *Men*, by the *Souls* of [*r*] *those who begat them*, by the *Souls* of their

[*r*] Gibraltar, *page* 12, line 20.

great

(s) Solon, page 38, line 2.

[t] Love the Leveller, page 13, line 24.

(u) The Faithful General, page 68. line 38.

[x] The Biter, page 19. line 27. p 25, 14. p 52, 1 20.

(y) The Biter, page 20, line 10.

(z) The Biter, page 53. line 23.

(a) The Female Wits, page 39, line 21,

(b) The Roving Husband reclaim'd, page 15, line 5.

(c) The Stage Coach, page 4, line 17,

(d) Ulysses, page 2, line 24.

(e) Matth. 5. 34. James 5. 12.

[s] *great Ancestors*, by their [t] *Fathers Tomb*, and [u] *injur'd Shade*, by the [x] *Majesty of Pekin* (in China) by the [y] *Great Lama* (in China) by the (z) *most potent and serene Cham*, in China, by their (a) *Hopes of Catiline*, by (b) *George*, by (c) *St. Patrick*, and by (d) *the Great Ulysses*. I really believe, that they had not invented so many, and such strange Sorts of *Oaths*; but only because our *Saviour* and St. *James* have forbidden them (e) to *swear at all*.

(f) See Pool's Synopsis, upon Gen. 42. 16.

(g) Eusebius *his* Ecclesiastical History, Book 4. Chap. 15.

It is generally owned by (f) *Commentators*, that *Joseph* sinned when he swore *by the life of Pharoah*, and that neither the Custom of the Place, nor the Vehemency of the Occasion could excuse the Fact. But it is most certain that (g) *Polycarp*, when he suffered Martyrdom, might have been released if he would have sworn *by the Fortune of Cæsar*, and gave this Reason for his Refusal; *If thou requirest this, Hear freely,*

freely, I am a Christian. However, the Reader need not wonder at these *Oaths,* if he peruseth (*h*) some other *Expressions* of the like Nature, mentioned in the Margin.

(*h*) Perolla and Izadora, page 4. line 27. p 27. l 7. p 62, l 27. Solon, page 19, line 14. Ulysses, page 2, line 5. p 39. l 3. p 52. l 11.

It was *Lucifer*'s Pride to affect a (*i*) likeness to *God,* for which he was cast out of *Heaven*; but now the Epithet [*] *Godlike* is frequently bestow'd by one *Actor* to another. I shall give some Instances of this Nature, out of the late Play, called *The British Enchanters.*

(*i*) *Isaiah* 14: 12, 13, 14.

[*] See Reference (*h*)

Page 11. line 23.

Like Mars *he look'd as Terrible and Strong,*
Like Jove *Majestick, like* Apollo *young*;
With all their Attributes divinely grac'd,
And sure their Thunder in his Arm was
[*plac'd.*

Page 35. line 3.

Were Amadis *restor'd to my Esteem,*
I could reject a Deity for him.

This is spoken of other Men, let us therefore see what an *Actor* saith of himself, *p.* 6, *l.* 23. *Our*

Our Priests have better learn'd what now
  is ill;
Can, when I please, be good; and none
  shall dare
Preach or expound, but what their King
  would hear.
Ere they interpret, let them mark my
  Nod,
My Voice their Thunder, this right Arm
  their God.

(*) The Loyal Subject, page 43, line 15. The Mistake, page 6, line 23. The NorthernLass, page 54, line *ult.*
[k] Love the Leveller, page 42, line 2.
(l) Solon, page 64. line 15.

And as they *swear* by Men; so they also frequently *swear* by Women; (*) *By our Lady,* or the *Virgin Mary;* (k) *By the Life of their dear Princess,* and (l) others present upon the *Stage :* Nay, the Expressions they use to Women favours of such *Blasphemy* as is dreadful to relate, and would be so resented in any Place but the *Stage,* where it passeth for *Fine Language;* of which I shall give some Instances.

Liberty Asserted, *page 25, line 29.*

——————— *Do I accept her ?*
With greater Rapture than the Wretch
  that's freed
From Death's convulsive Pangs embraceth
  Heav'n.

                                        'The

The Careless Husband, *p.* 35, *l.* 36.

You have fix'd me yours, to the last
Existence of my Soul's Eternal Entity.

The Confederacy *page* 28, *line* 28,
spoken of another Man's Wife.

Tell her, I am all Hers; Tell her, my
Body is Hers; Tell her, my Soul is Hers,
and tell her, my Estate is Hers.

I could fill several Pages with this *(m)* Abra-
Language; but he who desires more, Mule, *Epilogue*
may turn to the *(m)* Quotations in the page 1. line
Margin, where his Curiosity will be 6. p 3. l *pe-*
abundantly gratified. nult. p 4. l 9.
p 16. l 1.
Gibraltar,
page 58. line 12. *and* p 13. l 30. *spoken of an Intreaguing Pimp.*
Liberty Asserted, page 40. line 9. Love the Leveller, page 61,
line 31. p 63. l 7. p 65, l 11, 22. Solon, page 20. line 23. p 64.
l 15. The Amorous Miser, page 5. line 27. p 57. l 18. The British Enchanters, page 7. line 8 *and* 29. p 15. l 13. The Careless
Husband, page 27, line 33. p 65. l 1. The Conquest of Spain, page
12. line 5. The Fair Example, page 18. line 15. The Faithful
General, page 21. line 16. The Female Wits, page 54. line 23.
The Gamester, page 5. line 11. p 41. l 19. p 61. l. 1. The Lawyer's Fortune, p 16. line 28. p 46. l *penult.* The Portsmouth Heiress, page 56. line 12. *spoken by one in a Parson's Habit.* p 10. l 28. p
52. l 22. The Rival Brothers, page 6. line 27, *to* 37. p 15, l 19.
p 82. l 11. The Roving Husband Reclaim'd, page 47. line 14.
Zelmane, page 6. line 6. p 70. l 10.

The

The Words of an *antient Divine* (n) of this Nation are so remarkable concerning the *Play-House Oaths*, that I cannot forbear to repeat them at large. *How darest thou*, saith he, *whosoever thou art, to swear* by the Masse, by thy Faith, by thy Troth, by our Lady, by St. George *or the like ? Are these thy Gods whom thou hast made to serve them ? Or darest thou to give the worship due to God, unto any but unto him ?* Did the Lord threaten ruin upon Israel, *because they swore by their Idols in* Dan *and* Beersheba, *saying* (o) they that swear by the Sin of Samaria, and say, thy God, O Dan, liveth, and the manner of Beersheba liveth, even they shall fall, and never rise up again, *and darest thou swear* by the Masse, *which was the Sin of* England, *and is the Sin of* Rome ? *Did the Lord tell* Judah, *that* (p) her Children had forsaken him, because they swore by them that were no Gods ? *And darest thou swear* by our Lady, by St. George, by St. John, by St. Thomas, *or the like, which are no Gods ? Dost thou not see that thus swearing thou forsakest God, and bringest Ruin upon thy self ?* Did our blessed Saviour

tell

(n) Airay *upon the Philippians, chap.* I. *verse* 8. *page* 99, 100.

(o) Amos 8. 14.

(p) Jer. 5. 7.

tell the Scribes *and* Pharisees, *saying,* (q) Whosoever sweareth by the altar, sweareth by it, and by all things thereon: And whosoever sweareth by the temple, sweareth by it, and by him that dwelleth therein: And whosoever sweareth by heaven, sweareth by the throne of God, and by him that sitteth thereon? *and dost thou think that when thou swearest by thy* Faith, *thou swearest not by him in whom thou believest? Or when thou swearest by thy* Troth, *thou swearest not by him in whom thou trustest? &c. In one Word, thou that commonly swearest by any thing that is not* God, *tell me what thinkest thou? Dost thou therein swear by* God, *or no? If so, then* thou takest his Name in vain, and he will not hold thee guiltless. *If not, then thou forsakest* God, *in that thou swearest by that which is no* God.

There are three *Oaths* mention'd by this Reverend *Author* very common upon the *Stage,* namely their *Swearing* (r) by the *Mass,* (s) by their *Faith,* and (t) by their *Troth.* How scandalously the *Stage* is guilty may be seen from the following Margin. The

(q) Matth. 23. 20, 21, 22.

(r) The Loyal Subject, page 69, line 34. The Royal Merchant, page 29, line 25. p 30, l 20. p 51, l 4, *and* 15. p 54, l 13. *(s) By my* Faith. The

Confederacy, page 30, line 12. p 45, l 33. p 63, l 16. p 71 l 13.

F

The

The Loyal Subject, *page* 47. *line* 40. The Northern Lass, *page* 16. *line* 33. p. 41. l. 29. p. 60. l. 1. *Upon my Faith.* The Careless Husband, *page* 25. *line* 9. The Confederacy, *page* 22. *line* 29. The Northern Lass, *page* 27, *line* 36. *In good Faith.* Squire Trelooby, *page* 11. *line antepenult.* The Amorous Miser, *page* 12. *line* 27. p. 58. l. 25. The Lawyer's Fortune, *page* 49, *line* 17. The Northern Lass, *page* 30, *line antepenult.* *Good Faith!* Arsinoe, *page* 26. *line* 3. The Mistake, *page* 1, *line* 8. p. 7. l. 27. p. 16. l. 29. p. 53. l. 6. The Northern Lass, *page* 6. *line* 30. *Gude Feath.* The Northern Lass, *page* 19. *line* 9. p. 23. l. 24. *Feath.* The Northern Lass, *page* 18. *line* 33. p. 23. l. 20. p. 36. l. 33. *Faith and Troth.* Gibraltar, *page* 5. *line* 18. The Amorous Miser, *page* 3. *line* 24. p. 49. l. 1. p. 56. l. 22, 23, 24, 25. *four times in four lines.* The Biter, *page* 13. *line* 5. p. 14. l. 31. p. 55. l. 1. p. 56. l. 8. *I'faith,* The Gamester, *page* 44. *line* 14. *I'faith.* An Act at Oxford, *page* 46. *line* 2. Gibraltar, *page* 4. *line* 24. p. 6. l. 32. p. 23. l. 1. Sheet F p. 41. l. 15. Sheet F p. 44. l. 11, 30 and 37. Sheet G p. 51. l. 30. Hampstead Heath, *page* 52. *line* 3. Love at first Sight, *page* 23. *line* 5. p. 13. l. 9. p. 18. l. 27. p. 42. l. 17. p. 46. l. 29. p. 55. *Act* 5. l. 12. p. 66. l. 25. Love the Leveller, *page* 18. *line* 1. p. 24. l. *antepenult.* p. 51. l. 26. p. 58. l. 23. The Basset Table, *page* 44. *line* 27. p. 45. l. 25. The Biter, *page* 25. l. *ult.* The Confederacy, *page* 28. *line ult.* p. 43. l. 28. p. 49, l. 24. The Fair Example, *page* 1. l. *penult.* p. 39. l. 16. p. 65. l. *antepenult.* The Female Wits, *page* 17. *line* 16. p. 18. l. 8. The Gamester, *page* 63. l. 12. The Loyal Subject, *page* 44. *line* 35. The Metamorphosis, *page* 40. *line* 4. The Mistake, *page* 27. *line* 17. The Northern Lass, *page* 3. *line* 39. p. 5. l. 10. p. 17. l. 12. The Stage Coach, *page* 14. *line* 29.

(t) *By my Troth.* Gibraltar. Sheet G page 56. *line* 34. Love at first Sight, *page* 26. *line* 3. Love the Leveller, *page* 22. *line* 9. The Metamorphosis, *page* 29. *line antepenult.* The Mistake, *page* 16. *line* 18. The Northern Lass, *page* 19. *line* 7. p. 55. l. 19. The Roving Husband Reclaim'd, *page* 14. *line* 13. The Royal Merchant, *page* 35. *line* 6. *In Troth.* Gibraltar, *page* 16. *line* 30. Solon, *page* 14. *line ult.* Squire Trelooby, *page* 7. *line* 1. p. 9. l. *penult.* The Amorous Miser, *page* 44. *line* 9 and 19. The Gamester, *page* 4. *line* 2. The Loyal Subject, *page* 32. *line* 23. p. 43. l. 9. The Northern Lass, *page* 36. *line* 4 and 36. p. 39. l 21. p. 60. l. 15. The Rival Brothers *page* 22. *line* 11. *Upon my Troth.* The Loyal Subject, *page* 27. *line* 29. *Troth.* Fortune in her Wits, *page* 25. *line* 14. Solon, *page* 6. *line antepenult.* p. 53. l. 10. The Amorous Miser, *page* 33. *line* 3. The Fair Example, *page* 39. *line ult.* The

Female

Commonness of these *Oaths* takes off
the Sence of them, so that many
People are guilty of them, before they
are aware; and others think them to be
no *Sins* at all, but are very apt to excuse them and plead for them. However,
none of these external Circumstances
can alter the Nature of Good and E-
vil. *Vice* is not at all the better, tho'
it hath many Followers, and as many
to plead for it. What the *Scripture*
condemns, our pleading for it will
never excuse. The *Scripture* tells us
Matth. 12. 36. *that of every idle word
that men shall speak, they shall give an
account at the day of judgment*; and
this Text is of a greater Latitude in its
Meaning, than many imagine. Some
say, that these are not *Oaths*, but only
solemn Asseverations; tho' I must confess that a solemn Asseveration, by
any thing that is sacred, carrieth in it so
much of an *Oath*, that I know not how to
distinguish between them: And I must be
excus'd if I believe my Blessed *Saviour*
notwithstanding the Cavils, and frivolous Excuses of an Atheistical Age.

F 2   The

(u) An Act at Oxford, page 2. line 15. p. 7. l. 22. p. 28, l. 20. p. 49. l. 11. p. 52, l. 5. p. 54. l. 19. p 56. l. 7. Fortune in her Wits, page 6. line 18.

The Word (u) 'Faith, as it is frequently us'd by the *Stage* is an *Oath*, and the same as *by my Faith*, and yet of this there are near two Hundred Instances in our late *Plays*. That it is an *Oath* is evident, because in all Languages there is a Figure call'd *El-*

p 7. l 11. p 11. l 27. p 29. l 16. Gibraltar, page 1: line 4. p 3. l 32. p 8. l 5 and 36. p 15. l 22 and 27. p 18. l 4 and 13. p 19. l 22. p 20. l antepenult. p 21. l 11. p 24. l 28, 32 and penult. Sheet E p 33. l 6. Sheet E p 36. l 25 and 28. Sheet F p 46. l 30. Sheet F p 47. l 19. sheet G p 56. l 4. sheet I p 58. l 12 and 18. p 62. l 25. p 63. l 4. p 64. l 5. Hampstead Heath, p 9. l 29. p 18. l 30. p 32. l 1. p 55. l 12. p 57. l 17. Love at first Sight, page 2. line 27. p 3. l 34. p 5. l 16. p 43. l 3. p 55. Act 5. l 2. Love the Leveller, page 27 p 3. p 37. l 28. p 54. l ult. p 57. l 19. p 59. l 4. p 60. l antepenult. p. 61. l 5 and 30. Solon, page 10. line 15. Squire Trelooby, page 5. line 8. p 8, l 4 and 24. p 13. l 16. p 49. l 14. p 52. l 11. The Amorous Miser, Prologue, line 5. page 1. line 11. p 2. l 1. p 3. l 18. p 7. l 17. p 11 l 4 and 9. p 12. l 2 and 8. p 13. l 3. p 17. l 5. p 18. l 3, 7 and 19. p 27. line ult. p 31. l penult. p 42. l 1. p 44. l 7. p 45. l 1. p 49. l 11. p 53. l 19. p 54. l 23 and 25. p 55. l 30. p 59. l 5. The Basset Table, page 9. line penult. p 10. l antepenult. p 20. l 22. p 43. l 1. p 47. l 4. p 48. l 11. p 49. l 8 and 33. p 56. l 20. p 57. l ult. p ult. l 4. The Biter, page 16. line 33. p 23. l 16. p 25. l 1. p 36. l 4. p 51. l 17. p 61. l 15. The Careless Husband, page 3. line 8. The Cares of Love, page 15. line 35. p 42. l 10. p 48. l 2. The Confederacy, page 5. l 12. p 68. l penult. The Faithful General, Epilogue, line 20. The Female Wits, page 6. line 11. p 15. l 11 and 31. p 27. l 4. p 34. l 8. p 37. l 25. The Gamester. page 33. line 26. p 45. l 19. The Lawyer's Fortune, page 7. line 13. p 11. l 2. p 13. l 8. p 15. l 17. p 49. Scene 2. l 8. The Loyal Subject, page 47. line 38. p 48. l 7. p 53. l 4 and 11. The Lying Lover, page 2. line 8. p 3. l 21. p 20. l 6. p 26. l 6. p 38. l 8. p 44, l 33. p 50. l 17. The Metamorphosis, page 30. line 19. p 31, l 12. p 36, l 16. The Northern Lass, page 1, line 5. p 4, l 8. p 7, Scene 5, l 12. p 8, l 2, p 20, Scene 3, l 20. p 72, l 24.

The'

lipsis, which is spoken of in most *Grammars*. This is a Leaving out of some Words in a Sentence, which must be added to make the Sence compleat, and it is always imply'd, where the Sence is imperfect. Now the Word *Faith* standing thus alone is Nonsence, and therefore other Words are imply'd to make Sence of it; and if it is thus turn'd into Sence there is no Way to excuse it, from being an *Oath*. If it is objected, that the Word *'Faith* is no *Oath*, but the Words *by my Faith* are an *Oath*; I may affirm for the same Reason, that the Words of our *Saviour*, *Joh.* 17. 11. *Holy Father, keep those whom thou hast given me*, is no Prayer; but if it had been O *Holy Father*, then it had been a Prayer. According to the Scripture Interpretation, some particular Words may

F 3   be

be *Oaths*, tho' the *Formula jurandi*, these little Particles are left out, and must be supplied by the Figure *Ellipsis*. The Particles among the *Greeks* are either Μά or Νή. Now these are left out, in *Heb.* 6. 13. where *God* said to *Abraham, surely, blessing I will bless thee :* And yet it is here said that *God sware by himself*, because he *could swear by no greater*, and *confirm'd the truth of his promise with an oath.* The Word in *Greek* is Αμήν, *Amen*, and is reckon'd as an *Oath*, because it is one of the Names of *Christ*, who *Rev.* 3. 14. is call'd the *Amen, the faithful and true witness, the beginning of the creation of God.* If it is said, that in the Word *Faith* is not meant *God*, or *Christ* ; I must affirm that it is false. It plainly refers to the Object of our Faith, and consequently to every Person mention'd in our *Creed.* As therefore the *Jews*, when they *swore by the Temple*, or *by Heaven*, were guilty of *swearing by God*, who dwelt in the one, and whose Throne was in the other ; so *Christians*, when they *swear by their Faith*, are guilty of *swearing by* that *God* in whom they believe. Perhaps such an

Oath

Oath is not punished by the Laws of Man, tho' all *profane Oaths* are punishable; however, the Defect of our Laws, or Neglect of Execution, makes not the Sin the more excusable in the Sight of God; but when it is not punished by Men in this World, the God who will not hold such *Sinners* guiltless, seems to reserve the immediate Execution of Vengeance for himself in the other. And therefore, notwithstanding all their Excuses, the *Stage* is guilty in this, as well as in other *Oaths* of a more horrid Nature; insomuch, that we have Cause daily to pray to God, and say, *From such swearing and blasphemous Language, Good Lord deliver us.*

CHAP.

CHAP. III.

The Stage Guilty of Cursing.

PRofane *Cursing* is a *Sin* most positively forbidden by *God* in [a] the Holy *Scriptures*. Such *Language* ought not to proceed out of our Mouths, nor be harbour'd so much as [b] in our Thoughts. No (c) Provocation whatsoever will excuse it. We must not *curse* even those who *curse* us, who are our *Enemies*, who *hate* us, who *despightfully use* us, and *persecute* us. We must not imitate such but *God*, who continully poureth out his *Blessings* upon all. We must *not render evil for evil, or railing for railing, but contrari- wise blessing ; as knowing that we are cal- led* of God *to inherit a blessing :* And thus must we *overcome evil with good*. It was therefore foolish Advice which was given to *Job* in his Afflictions, (d) that he should *Curse God and die*, and it was resented accordingly. This *Sin* in some Cases among the *Jews* was a (e) *capital Crime*, and the Son of *Shelomith*, by the Command of *God* was stoned for the same. When (f) *Shimei.*

[a] *Rom.* 12. 14. *James* 3. 9, 10.

[b] *Job* 31. 30. *Eccles.* 10. 20.

(c) *Rom.* 12. 14. *Matth* 5. 44, 45. *Luk.* 6. 28. 1 *Pet.* 3. 9, 10. *Rom.* 12. 21.

(d) *Job* 2. 9, 10.

(e) *Exod.* 21. 17. *Levit.* 20. 9.

(f) 2 *Sam.* 16. 5, 6, 7, 10. *& Chap.* 19. 23.

Shimei cursed David, tho whilst he lived, he forgave the *Sin,* as against himself, yet he would not pass it by, as it related to *God,* or might have been of ill Consequence to the Nation; but he gave Orders at his Decease, that (g) the Man who thus *cursed,* should be put to Death, which were executed accordingly. Nay in such Cases as were not punished by Man, *God* himself was the Executioner of his Wrath upon them that were guilty; and therefore *David* saith (h) that *for the sin of their mouth, and for the words of their lips, they shall be taken in their pride; and for cursing and lying which they speak,* and tells us the sad Estate of such a *Sinner,* that (i) *As he loved cursing, so it shall come unto him; as he delighted not in blessing, so it shall be far from him. As he cloathed himself with cursing like as with a garment; so it shall come into his bowels like water, and like oyl into his bones. It shall be unto him as the garment which covereth him, and for a girdle wherewith he is girded continually.* When *Goliah* (k) *cursed David,* he and the whole Army were afterward destroy'd; and Vengeance seems to be but

the

(g) 1 *Kings* 2. 8, 9, 44, 45, 46.

(h) *Psal.* 59. 12.

(i) *Psal.* 109. 17, 18, 19. *The Verbs in Hebrew are in the future Tense; and therefore these Verses contain rather a Prophesy than an Imprecation.*

(k) 1 *Sam.* 17. 43, 49, 50, 51.

the natural Effect of such Imprecations.
(*l*) Pfal. The *Curse* of *God* is a dreadful thing.
37. 22. As (*l*) *such* who *are bleſſed of him ſhall*
(*m*) Matth. *inherit the land*; ſo *they who are cur-*
25. 41, 46. *ſed ſhall be rooted out.* Nay ſhall (*m*)
(*n*) Pfal. *be caſt into the fire prepared for the*
10. 7. Rom. *Devil and his Angels.* He therefore
3. 14, 18. (*n*) *whoſe mouth was full of curſing*
(*o*) Numb. *and bitterneſs,* was always reckon'd as
23. 8. a wicked Man, and one who had *no fear*
of God before his *eyes.* To this, I
may add, that *Balaam,* (*o*) who was a
notorious *Enchanter,* and who *loved the*
wages of unrighteouſneſs, dar'd not be
guilty of it, tho he might receive his
Houſe full of Silver *and* Gold as a
Reward; and therefore refus'd it,
without a ſpecial Leave from *God*
himſelf, which never was granted.
How, ſaith he, *ſhall I curſe them, whom*
God hath not curſed? and how ſhall I defy
them, whom the Lord hath not defied?

This being therefore conſider'd, it
is dreadful even to relate; how horridly the *Actors* on the *Stage* are
guilty in this Reſpect, and in what
direct Oppoſition they ſet themſelves
to the Word of *God,* and the Exerciſe
of Religion. In the *Church* we pray to
God, that *his Name may be Hallowed*; In
the

the *Play-Houſe* it is profaned by bitter *Oaths* and *Curſes*. In the *Church* we are taught *not to take the name of the Lord our God in vain, becauſe he will not hold ſuch* Sinners *guiltleſs* : In the *Play-Houſe* his Name is ſpoken in Deriſion, and he is call'd upon to do his worſt. In the *Church* we profeſs to believe that *God* is *Almighty* : In the *Play-Houſe* he is petition'd to pour out the fierceſt of his Wrath and Indignation upon them ; as if *Heav'n* was to be deſpis'd, and *Hell* and *Damnation* rather to be deſir'd.

Sometimes the *Actors curſe themſelves,* if that is not true which they ſay, or if they perform not their Promiſe. In ſuch Caſes they wiſh that they may (*p*) *be damn'd*, (*q*) *die*, or (*r*) *rot*, (*s*) *be hang'd*, (*t*) *confounded*, (*u*) *ſtricken blind*, or (*x*) *ſtupid*, that the

(*p*) The Roving Husband Reclaim'd, *page* 11. *line* 14. p 38, l 19. The Stage Beaux toſs'd in a Blanket, *page* 15, *line* 1.

(*q*) The Stage Beaux toſs'd in a Blanket, *page* 4, *line* 30. p 5, l 15 *and* 42. p 6, l 9. p 14, l 2. p 16, l 25. p 19, l 6. p 43, l *antepenult.* p 44, l 10 *and* 26. p 57, l 1 *and* 32. p 58, l 18, *penult and ult.* p 59, l 23 *and* 25.

(*r*) The Roving Husband Reclaim'd, *page* 56, *line* 21. The Stage Beaux toſs'd in a Blanket, *page* 8, *line* 25. p 9, l 6.

(*s*) Love at firſt Sight, *page* 4, *line* 4. Solon, *page* 2, *line* 13. The Loyal Subject, *page* 4, *line* 35.

(*t*) The Female Wits, *page* 43, *line* 13.

(*u*) The Careleſs Husband, *page* 19, *line* 12

(*x*) The Careleſs Husband, *page* 34, *line* 10.

Dewce

(y) The Basset Table, page 24, line 30. p 32, l 20. The Careless Husband, page 5, line 28. p 6, l antepenult.

(z) The Careless Husband, page 3, line 19. The Confederacy, page 16, line 5.

Dewee may (y) *take*, or (z) *fetch them*, that (a) *the Devil may blow their Heads off*, may (b) *burn them*, may (c) *choak them*, may (d) *drive them*, (e) *upon a Red Herring*, may (f) *fetch them*, and (g) *take them*, that (h) *Heav'n may curse them*, (i) *the Sun may burn them*, (k) *Curse may catch them*, (l) *Hell may take them*, and (m) *their Breath may be stop'd*. One (n) wishes, that *the four Winds may conspire his eternal Disorder*, another that (o) *Dogs and Kites may eat*

(a) The Basset Table, page 53, line 6.

(b) The Roving Husband Reclaim'd, page 15. line 26.

(c) The Stage Beaux toss'd in a Blanket, Prologue line ult.

(d) The Careless Husband, page 16, line antepenult.

(e) An Act at Oxford, page 58, line 30.

(f) The Confederacy, page 66, line 32.

(g) Love at first Sight, page 56, line 12. Squire Trelooby, page 5, line 22. p 9, l 15. The Basset Table, page 12, line 9. The Stage Beaux toss'd in a Blanket, page 8. line 32.

(h) The Royal Merchant, page 49, line 6.

(i) The Careless Husband, page 18, line 38.

(k) The Careless Husband, page 32, line 10.

(l) The Loyal Subject, page 57, line 28.

(m) The Careless Husband, page 20, line 1. p 52, l 15. p 65, l 37.

(n) An Act at Oxford, page 9, line 8. Hampstead Heath, page 11. line 17.

(o) The Loyal Subject, page 65, line 3.

up-

up his Heart, and another, that (*p*) the *Eternal Frowns of all the* Female Sex *may doubly damn him*; as if the Difpleafure of his *Miftrefs* was a greater Torment than the Lofs of *God* and *Heav'n.* Nay the Conditions, upon which thefe *Horrid Imprecations* are grounded, are oftentimes broken upon the *Stage,* and then they contain an absolute *Curfe* without any Reftriction. Thus (*q*) the *Ld. Worthy* curfeth himfelf.

May I become the very'ft Wretch a-live, and all the Ills imaginable fall up-on my Head, if ever I fpeak to her, [the Lady Reveller] *more*; and yet they (*r*) afterward meet, and are [*s*] join'd in Marriage at the end of the *Play.*

In the *Gamefter, Valere* wifh'd, that when ever he play'd with the *Dice* again, [*t*] *all the Curfes rank'd with An-gelica's Difdain might purfue him*; and yet he was [*u*] afterward guilty, even [*x*] with *Angelica* her felf in Difguife, and in the End [*y*] the Difdain is turn'd to *Marriage.*

In the *Comedy* call'd *The Miftake,* [*z*] *Leonora* wifheth, that *if fhe begs Pardon of* Carlos, *Heav'n may never pardon her*; and *Carlos* fpeaks in more

dread-

(*p*) The Carelefs Husband, *page* 45, *line* penult.

(*q*) The Baffet Table *page* 14, *line* 32.

(*r*) The Baffet Table *page* 39 *and* 56. [*s*] *Page* 62.

[*t*] *Page* 25, *line* 23.

[*u*] *Page* 50. [*x*] *Page* 53. [*y*] *Page* 67.

[*z*] *Page* 40. *line* 9.

[a] *Ibid. line 14.* dreadful *Language*, [a] I *assure you with Heav'n and with Hell for seconds, for may the Joys of one fly from me, whilst the Pains of t'other overtake me, if ever I see you more:* Nay he goes

[b] *Page 41, line 22.* farther yet, [b] *may I starve, perish, rot, be blasted, dead, damn'd, or any other thing that Men or Gods can think on, if on any Occasion whatever, I from this Moment change one Word or Look*

[c] *Page 43, and 44.* *with you;* and yet they [c] meet afterward on the *Stage*, as familiarly as ever.

I weary the Reader with this *Hellish Language*, and therefore I shall

[d] *Page 49, Sheet I, line 12.* add but [d] one Quotation more, of this Nature, out of the same *Comedy*. *I imprecate,* saith Lorenzo, *the utmost Pow'rs of Heav'n to shower upon my Head the Deadliest of its Wrath, I ask that all Hells Torments may unite, to wound my Soul with an eternal Anguish, if wicked* Leonora *ben't my Wife.* To this Leonora answers. *Why then! may all those Curses pass him by, and wrap me in their everlasting Pains, if ever once I had a fleeting Thought of making him my Husband.*

This is strange Diversion for a *Christian Stage*, especially for *Comedy*;
and

and yet the half is not discover'd. The *Actors curse* themselves without any Restriction, that they may [e] *be damn'd* [f] *dye*, and [g] *rot*. Sometimes they wish that [h] *some Whirlwind* may *bear them thence*, that [i] *the Earth* may *open her Mouth, and swallow them up*, that they may [k] *have the Pox,* [l] *Lightning* may *blast* them, [m] *the Dewce* may *take* them, [n] *Perdition* may *seize* them, [o] *Curse* may *catch* them, [p] *Perdition, Shame and Disappointment* may *confound* them, [q] *Vengeance* may *choak* them, [r] their

[e] Love at first Sight, page 16, line 21. The Biter, page 13, line 30. The Female Wits, page 25, line 4. The Lawyer's Fortune, page 38, line 13. The Stage Beaux toss'd in a Blanket, page 11, line 9. P 31, l 25.

[f] Love at first Sight, page 37, line 1, 9, 26, 39 and ult. p 58, l 3, 17 and 22. p 60, l 31. p 61, l 7. p 62, l 4, 37 and ult. p 63, l 6. p 64, l 2, 14, 21, 32 and penult. p 65, l 37. p 67, l 33. p 68, l 3. The Stage Beaux toss'd in a Blanket, page 5, line 5 and 11. p 7, l 21. p 11, l 11. p 12, l 26. p 16, l 29. p 17, l 14, 21 and 26. p 19, l 6, 15 and 26. p 20, l 25. p 27, l 13. p 31, l 7. p 44, l 17. p 45, l 21. p 46, l 1. p 51, l 12. p 52, l 12 and 27. p 54, l 14. p 56, l 10. p 57, l 1. p 58, l 12 and 17. p 59, l 23 and 24.

[g] The Confederacy, page 67, line 28. The Stage Beaux toss'd in a Blanket, page 8, line 29 and antepenult. p 10, l 28. p 21, l antepenult. p 36, l 31. p 43, l 19. p 51, l antepenult.

[h] Fortune in her Wits, page 56, line 12. The British Enchanters, page 32, line 1.

[i] The British Enchanters, page 32, line 2.

[k] Gibraltar, page 2, line 28.

[l] Liberty Asserted, page 51, line 12.

[m] Squire Trelooby, page 36, line 8.

[n] Perolla and Izadora, page 12, line 8.

[o] The Careless Husband, page 19, line 3.

[p] The Portsmouth Heiress, page 71, line 9.

[q] The Fair Example, page 66, line 18.

[r] The Careless Husband, page 28, line 35.

Breath

[s] The
Amorous Mi-
ser, *page* 49,
line 23.

[t] The
Portsmouth
Heiress, *page*
54. *line* 22.

[u] Love at
first Sight,
page 25, *line*
10.

Breath may be *stopt*. and [s] their *Family* may be *hang'd*. One [t] curses
the *Stars which rul'd at* his *Nativity*,
and [u] another wishes that the *Curse*
may light *upon* him, because he is sick.
The *Damn'd* in *Hell* are not arriv'd to
this Wickedness. Tho' they *blaspheme*,
yet they dare not call for more *Curses*
upon their Heads. They know, to
their eternal Sorrow, what a dreadful
thing the *Curse* of *God* is; and had
our *Actors* but the Faith of *Devils*,
they would certainly tremble at that,
which they now make their constant
Diversion.

And now, since they thus *curse themselves* it cannot be wonder'd at that
they so frequently *curse* others. *The
Loyal Subject* [x] run's on with most
dreadful *Imprecations* of this Nature,
in eight and Twenty Lines together,
and [y] another in two and Twenty,
as if the *Poets* and *Actors* strove to out-
vye each other in this *dreadful Language*.
The Instances of this Nature are too
many to be transcrib'd, and of too
great a Variety to be reduc'd into
Order. Besides I must forbear, lest I
surfeit the *Reader*. However, he who
would view them in their proper Soil,
                                      may

[x] *Page*
12, *line* 32.
&c.

[y] Abra-
Mule, *page* 29.
line 1. &c.

may turn to the [z] Quotations men-tion'd in the Margin.

[z] An Act at Oxford, *page* 1, *line* 1. p. 16. *l.* 14.

p. 19. *l.* 30. *p* 23. *l.* 9. *p.* 22. *l.* penult. p. 24, *l.* 11, 17 *and* 25. p. 31. *l.* 14. *p.* 34, *Act* 4. *l.* 14. *p* 54, *l* 4. *p* 58, *l* 33. Fortune in her Wits, *page* 4, *line* 9. *p* 5, *l* 5. *p* 14. *l* ult. *p* 54. *l* 5, 6 *and* 11. Gibraltar, *page* 12, *line* 27 *and* ult. *p* 16, *l* 35. *p* 20, *l* 25. Sheet E *p* 33. *l* 1. Sheet E *p* 40. *l* 23. Sheet F *p* 41, *l* 6 *and* 26. *p* 63. *l* 20. *p* 54. *l* 21. *p* 68. *l* 3 *and* 21. Hampstead Heath, *page* 22. *line* 7. *p* 25. *l* 15 *and* 28. *p* 35. *l* 7. *p* 39. *l* 14. Liberty Asserted, *page* 5c. *line* 38. Love at first Sight, *page* 7. *line* 16. *p* 12. *l* 9. *p* 13. *l* 5. *p* 15. *l* 28. *p* 16. *l* 7 *and* 8. *p* 29. *l* 16. *p* 42. *l* 24. *p* 47. *l* 2. *p* 51. *l* 7. *p* 52. *l* 5. Love the Leveller, *page* 8. *line* 3 *and* 18. *p* 22. *l* 6. *p* 39. *l* 11. *p* 57. *l* 6. Perolla and Izadora, *page* 12. *line* 3 *and* 11. *p* 47. *l* 7. Solon, *page* 14. *Scene* 3. *line* 5. *p* 63. *l* 9. *p* 69. *l* 11. Squire Trelooby, *page* 5. *line* 16. *p* 26. *l* 13. The Cares of Love, *page* 4. *line* 4. *p* 13. *l* 20. *p* 36. *l* 7. *p* 41. *l* 15. *p* 47. *l* 24. *p* 48. *l* 5. *p* 49. *l* 17. The Confederacy, *page* 2. *line* 25. *p* 19. *l* 34. *p* 31. *l* 2. *p* 40. *l* 29. *p* 45. *l* 31. *p* 59. *l* 8 *and* 12. The Conquest of Spain, *page* 5. *line* 6. *p* 19. *l* antepenult. *p* 20. *l* 1. The Fair Example, *page* 24. *line* 2. *p* 25. *l* 18. *p* 35. *l* 14 *and* 25. The Female Wits, *page* 4. *line* 28. *p* 12. *l* 26. *p* 19. *l* 17. *p* 56. *l* 15. *p* 57. *l* 22. *p* 64. *l* 5. *p* 65. *l* 12. *p* 66. *l* 2. The Gamester, *page* 29. *line* 9. *p* 31. *l* 32. *p* 32. *l* 2. *p* 45. *l* penult. *p* 54. *l* 30. *p* 68. *l* 17. *p* 69. *l* 7. The Lawyer's Fortune, *page* 14. *line* 18. The Loyal Subject, *page* 39. *l* 42. *p* 73. *l* 30. The Portsmouth Heiress, *page* 14. *line* 19. *p* 21. *l* 24. *p* 53. *l* antepenult. *p* 70. *l* ult. The Roving Husband Reclaim'd, *page* 5. *line* 5. *p* 15. *l* 4. *p* 16. *l* 16. *p* 21. *l* 23. The Royal Merchant, *page* 25, *line* 17. *p* 32. *l* 1. *p* 49. *l* 6. *p* 55. *l* 27. *p* 56. *l* 23. The Stage Beaux toss'd in a Blanket, *Prologue*, *page* 2. *line* 15. The Stage Coach, *page* 1. *line* 4. *p* 2. *l* 6. *p* 16. *l* 19. *p* 21. *l* antepenult. *p* 26. *l* 16. The Tender Husband, *page* 29. *line* 18. *p* 58. *l* 21. Ulysses, *page* 45. *line* 5, 29 *and* 32. Zelmane, *page* 5. *line* 14. *p* 32. *l* antepenult.

I shall only observe, that in the *Plays* Printed in the Years 1704, and 1705, until the tenth Day of *March* last, there are near Fourteen Hundred Instances of *Swearing, Cursing* and *Blasphemy :*

G   These

These *Plays* are first acted several
Times near the City of *London,* and
afterward by the other Emissaries,
who wander through the Nation for
this Purpose. The *Play-Houses* near
London act several Nights in each
Week, especially in the Winter Season, before a great Concourse of People. A Thousand of these *Plays* are
afterward Printed to propagate their
Profaneness. Now as Men are the most
apt of all living Creatures to imitate
each other in that which is Evil, and
in that especially which is proposed
as a Diversion, and the Fashion of
the Age; so the *Reader* may judge
what a Deluge of *Impiety* flows from
these Fountains, sufficient, without an
interposing Providence, to overflow
the Nation, destroy the Vitals of *Religion,* and provoke *God* to turn his
Mercies into Judgments. To prevent
the ill Consequence hereof, let us pray
to *God,* like *David,* [†] *Tho' they curse,
yet bless thou :* And thus let us [*] *stand
in the gap, to turn away his wrathful
indignation, that we perish not.*

[†] *Psal.* 109.
28.
[*] *Psal.* 105.
23.

CHAP.

CHAP. IV.

Religion undermin'd and the Scriptures burlesqu'd by the Stage.

IT is easy to prove from the Instances of *Swearing*, *Cursing* and *Blasphemy* mention'd in the former Chapters, that the Design of the present *Stage* is to undermine *Religion*, and render both the sacred Majesty of *God* and his Judgments contemptible; but leaving the *Reader* to make his own *Reflections* hereon, I shall proceed to other Particulars, which have the same Tendency.

First therefore, That the *Players* may strike effectually at the Root of all *Religion*, they represent all Pretenders to it, as the most *wicked* Persons upon Earth, and scruple nothing which may serve to blacken their Character. They tell us such are notoriously guilty of (*a*) *Lying*, (*b*) *Abusing their Apprentices*, (*c*) made up of *Religion* and *Pride*, (*d*) will not touch a *Card*, for Fear of the *Devil*, and yet are always *swearing*, *cursing* and *hecto-*

(*a*) An Act at Oxford, page 9. line 33.
(*b*) An Act at Oxford, page 12, line penult.
(*c*) An Act at Oxford, page 42, line 12. Hampstead Heath, page 47, line 5.

(*d*) An Act at Oxford, and Hampstead Heath, *ibid.*

G 2　　　　　*ring*

ring in the Family. *The Noise of such an House,* say the Actors, *is* (e) *a perfect Nusance, for the whole Family are either swearing, or singing of Psalms.* Certainly they who pray and sing Hymns to the *Devil*, are offended because others pray to *God*, and sing Psalms to his Glory; and therefore they expose the one, that they may the better establish the other. In one *Comedy* (f) an *Actor* tells another, that such a Person *prays* much, to which this Answer is immediately return'd, *That's a bad Sign, A Religious Cloak is the best Covert for Infirmities.* Other Instances (g) of the same Nature might be added, if these were not sufficient. I pray *God* to deliver us in his due Time from such *Blasphemous Language*, but now (h) *Religion* is represented as a Cloak for *wickedness,* (i) *God* is describ'd as the Author of *Sin*, particulary of *Adultery*, and (k) the *Devil* as one who assists us in our just Designs. (l) The *Zeal* to save Souls is curs'd, (m) Preaching the Word of *God* exposed,

(e) An Act at Oxford, and Hampstead Heath, *ibid.*

(f) Love at first Sight, *page* 19, *line* 35.

(g) Love at first Sight, *page* 48, *line* 24. The Stage Beaux toss'd in a Blanket, *p. ult. in fine.*

(h) Gibraltar, *page* 8, *line* 19. The Portsmouth Heiress, *page* 6, *line* 4. The Roving Husband reclaim'd, *page* 13, *line* 10.

(i) The Roving Husband, reclaim'd, *pa.* 59, *line* 7.

(k) The British Enchanters, *page* 30, *line* 30.

(l) The Stage Beaux toss'd in a Blanket, *Prologue*, *page* 2, *line* 15.

(m) Solon, *page* 26, *line* 31. The Basset Table, *page* 3, *line* 8. *p.* 48, *l.* 10. The Rival Brothers, *Epilogue in fine*

all

all (*o*) that is spoken by a Man full of Intreagues seems like a Sermon, nay, (*p*) the very Reading of a Sermon in private, is as bad as Reading of a Bill for Mony, when there is nothing to pay it. (*q*) *Heav'n, Paradise* and *immortal Joys* are debased into an *Amour* to be enjoy'd in this Life; and accordingly, the *Religion* of the *Players* is sunk a Degree lower than that of *Mahomet*. When they speak of the Immortality of the Soul, they speak like *Atheists*; but when they speak of Enjoyments below, they speak like *Devils*. *Rhoderique* the King speaks on one Occasion, (*r*)

Who can resolve me what's beyond this Span?
Perhaps I may return to my first nothing.

and *Frontenac* Governour of *New France* speaks on the other, (*s*)

I am a God if nothing intervene,
To interrupt this more than mortal Joy.

(*o*) The *Tender Husband, page* 25, *line* 29.

(*p*) The *Confederacy page* 11. *line* 27.

(*q*) *Gibraltar, page* 49, *Sheet* H. *line* 27. *Liberty* asserted, *page* 26, *line* 29. *p.* 39, *l.* 15. *p.* 40. *l.* 11. *p.* 49, *l.* 30. *Love at first Sight, page* 17, *line* 7. *p.* 52, *l.* 8. The *Conquest of Spain, page* 54, *line* 37. The *British Enchanters, page* 14, *line* 2. *p.* 35, *line* 3. The *Loyal Subject, page* 44, line 18. The *Mistake, page* 36, *line* 26. The *Portsmouth Heiress, page* 11. *line* 5.

(*r*) The *Conquest of Spain, page* 66, *line* 22.
(*s*) *Liberty* Asserted, *page* 65, *line* 1.

In

(t) The Faithful General, *page* 32, *line* 46.

In one *Comedy* (t) *Heav'n* is repreſented as not worth the Abiding there with an Enemy; in (u) another *Everlaſting Reſt* is deſcrib'd by *ſinking* into the Grave, *and never Thinking again.* In another (x) an *Actor* tells a Story notoriouſly

(u) Ulyſ-ſes, *page* 36, *line* 4.

(x) The Lawyers Fortune, *pa.* 14, *line* 2.

falſe, and add's, *As I hope to be ſav'd 'tis true.* Some Suiters going from their Miſtreſſes call it (y) their *Everlaſting Leave,* and bid them (z) *eternally adieu,* and another (a) ſpeaks

(y) The Gameſter *pa.* 60, *line* 4.

(z) The Gameſter *pa.* 67, *line* 1.

fully on this Occaſion.

(a) The Britiſh Enchanters, *page* 7, *line* 29.

So much, ſo tenderly, your Slave adores,
He hath no Thought of happineſs but yours.

(b) An Act at Oxford, *page* 29, *line* 30. Hampſtead Heath, *page* 33. *line* 17. The Amorous Miſer, *page* 15, *line* 20. The Conſederacy, *pa.* 55, *line* 16. The Loyal Subject, *page* 31, *line antepenult.*

Beſides, The Torment of *Hell* is (b) made a Jeſt of, in Words too ſcandalous to be related, and whilſt the *Devils believe and tremble,* the *Actors* ridicule it. *A Damn'd Play* is ſuch a one as hath not *Profaneneſs* enough in it to pleaſe the Hearers, and this is an *Epithet* which they alſo uſe on other (c) Occaſions. What all this tends to except the utter exſtinguiſhing all Notions of future Rewards and Puniſh-

The Stage Beaux toſs'd in a Blanket, *Prologue, page* 3. *line* 6. *p.* 13, *l.* 18. The Lying Lover, *page* 20, *line* 5.

ments,

ments, I cannot imagine. Perhaps this Apprehension may keep People from the *Play-House*, and therefore they must remove the *Stumbling-Block* out of the Way.

To do this more effectually, they undervalue that *God* who doth reward and punish; not only in such Expressions as these,

(d) *You alone* [a Lady's waiting Gentlewoman] *can help to ease my Pain.*

(d) Arsinoe, *page* 7, *line* 2.

(e) *All other Losses I can bear;*
For he alone [a Lover] *is worth my Care.*

(e) Arsinoe, *page* 25, *in fine.*

(f) *Chiefly do I owe my Preservation to* Mars *my Guardian God.*

(f) Fortune in her Wits, *page* 17. *line* 6.

but in (g) another *Comedy* his Mercy is droll'd upon, and urged as an Argument for our Security in *Sin*: And in others his inestimable Love in the *Redemption* of the World by *Christ Jesus* is ridicul'd, and the Offices of our *Blessed Saviour* strangely undervalued. A General is saluted with (h) *All hail Triumpher, Saviour of the State, Cupid* (i) is represented as a *Mediator* between Man and Wife, like

(g) The Mistake *pa.* 44, *line* 15.

(h) The Faithful General, *page* 3, *line* 30.

(i) The Portsmouth Heiress, *page ult, line* 24.

G 4   *Christ*

Christ between *God* and *Man*, and the Word *Mediator* printed at large in a different Character, that it may be the more taken Notice of. One asks (*k*) *Must I go into that nasty Hole which I call'd by way of Joke the Gate of Hell?* And the Answer is immediately return'd, *Even thither until you are redeem'd.* The *Actors* tells us that (*l*) *Play Mony is a sacred thing, and not to be profaned,* and I wish they would observe the same Rule in such things as relate to *God,* the *Scriptures* and *Religion.*

I doubt I shall be too tedious in Representing their *horrid* Burlesquing of the *Holy Scriptures,* and therefore I shall omit such Passages as have been already taken Notice of, and only touch upon some others. To make sure Work of the whole ; (*m*) when an *Actor* tells a most notorious Lye, it is with this Asseveration that *it is as true as the Gospel.*

But to be more Particular.

The *Scripture* tells us, that (*n*) *In the beginning God created the heaven and the earth* The *Actors* (*o*) ridicule the Word *Creature* as if they believed no such thing, but that either the World was
eternal

(*k*) Fortune in her Wits, *page* 20, *line* 26.
(*l*) The Confederacy, *page* 15. *line* 32.

(*m*)Squire Trelooby, *page* 40, *line* 17.

(*n*) Gen. 1. 1.
(*o*) The Tender Husband, *page* 20, *line* 25.

eternal or made by an accidental Concourse of *Atoms. Creature! What! your own Cousin a Creature! What!— a Creature! nay, now I am sure you are ignorant.*

The *Scripture* tells us, that (*p*) the Serpent, or the Devil, *was more subtil than any beast of the earth, which the Lord had made,* and that he continues a cunning Adversary with various Wiles and Devices; an *Actor* (*q*) tells a Woman, *Sure the Serpent parted with his Subtilty, and clos'd in the Fruit he gave thy Sex.*

The *Scripture* tells us (*r*) that *God open'd the mouth of* Balaam's *ass;* the Players burlesque the Story, *An* (*s*) *Ass hath spoken at a less Injury than this.*

In the *Scripture,* God (*t*) positively forbids *the woman to wear that which appertaineth to a man,* and also *the man* to *put on a womans apparel,* and gives this Reason, *for all that do so are an abomination to the Lord.* The Players often transgress this Command for the sake of the Jest, where sometimes (*u*) Women, and sometimes (*x*) Men are guilty in this Particular.

(*p*) *Gen.* 3. 1.

(*q*). The Portsmouth, Heiress, *page* 70, *line* 1.

(*r*) *Numb.* 22. 28.

(*s*) The Portsmouth, Heiress, *page* 47, *line* 28.

(*t*) *Deut.* 22. 5.
(*u*) Gribraltar, *page* 44, *Sheet* F. *line* 32. *p* 55. *Sheet* G. *line* l. 3. The Gamester, *pa.* 53, *line* 15. The Mistake, *Dramatis Personæ* Women *line* 2. The Tender Husband, *Dramatis Personæ,* Fainlove *sere per totum.*

(*x*) Gibraltar, *page* 47, *Sheet* F. *line* 8. Squire Trelooby, *page* 47.

In

In Scripture, *David* speaking of his Death as near, saith (y) *I go the way of all the earth.* This Text in the *Play-House* is [z] ridiculously applied to *carnal Copulation.*

In the Scripture, *David* saith (a) *I will praise thee, O God, for I am fearfully and wonderfully made; marvellous are thy works, and that my soul knoweth right well;* the *Players* express it thus (b) *The blind Work of Chance which produced a Monster.*

In Scripture, *Solomon* tells us (c) that *To every thing there is a season, and time for every purpose under the sun;* this Expression the *Players* repeat, and make a *Blasphemous Inference,* that (d) therefore *a Bottle is good in the Evening, and a Whore doth well in the Morning.*

These are excellent Comments on the *Old Testament,* and upon Enquiry we shall find that the *New* fares no better.

In the *New Testament* we are often commanded, to [e] *repent* and turn from Sin that we may be fit for the Promises of the Gospel. The *Players* tell us, that this is not worth our while, and that he who [f] marries,

that

(y) 1 Kings 2. 2.

[z] The Stage Coach, page 12. line 21.

(a) Psal. 139. 14.

(b) The Female Wits, page 62, line 16.

(c) Eccles 3. 1.

(d) Gibraltar, page 39, Sheet E. line 37.

[e] Matth. c. 2 and 4. 17. Mark 1. 15 and 6. 12. Luke 13. 3. Acts 2. 38 and 3. 19 and 17. 30. and 26. 20.

[f] Gibraltar, page 38, Sheet E. line 7.

that he may afterward live honeſt, makes a bad Bargain, ſince he *purchaſeth a ſhort Pleaſure, with a long Repentance, and the loſs of Liberty.*

Our *Bleſſed Saviour* [h] is very particular in forbidding us to commit *Adultery,* ſaying that to this end we ſhould avoid every Provocation thereto; for *he who looketh on a woman to luſt after her, hath committed adultery with her already in his heart*: But if we ſhould have ſuch Inclinations, tho' they are as dear to us as an *Eye* or a *Foot,* yet he commands us to part with them under the Penalty of *Hell Fire.* The *Players* tell us, if we have a luſtful Thought, we may go on to the utmoſt. (*i*) For, they ſay, *what ſignifies a Woman's being Chaſt in the Fleſh if ſhe is a Whore in her Spirit: And to what Purpoſe is it to keep her ſelf from the World, if ſhe has ſuffer'd her ſelf beforehand to be debauch'd by the Devil?*

Our *Bleſſed Saviour* exhorts us (*k*) that *whatſoever we would that men ſhould do to us, we ſhould do ſo to them;* this Text is uſed by the *Players* (*l*) in Vindication of Adultery.

Our *Bleſſed Saviour* (*m*) ſaith in Matters of *Religion* there muſt be no Neutrality.

[h] *Mat.* 5. 27, 28, 29.

(*i*) Gibraltar, *page* 3. *line* 34.

(*k*) *Matth.* 7. 12.

(*l*) Gibraltar, *page* 16. *line* 14.

(*m*) *Matth.* 12. 30.

Neutrality. The *Players* jest with this Expression. (*n*) *He*, saith one in a Captain's Habit, *that is not for us is against us, therefore plunder.*

Our *Blessed Saviour* (*o*) commands us to *render unto Cesar the things which are Cesar's, and unto God the things which are God's ;* this Text is applied by the *Stage* to encourage Whoring. It is but laying the Child to the right Father. But, (*p*) saith an Actress, *if I receive their Flames, what if I should grow soft upon it, and receive a dangerous Impression ?* To this it is answered, *Why then you must be render'd to the Man whose Image you bear,* concluding with an Exhortation to fear nothing.

(*o*) *Matth.* 22. 21.

(*p*) The Portsmouth Heiress, page 19. line 14.

Our *Blessed Saviour* (*q*) tells us a Parable of *Lazarus,* that *he desired to be fed with the crumbs that fell from the rich man's table,* and was afterwards *carried by the angels into Abraham's bosom.* To ridicule the first Expression, (*s*) *What*, saith an *Actor, would those poor Ladies that are confin'd at Court, give for the Crumbs of Lovers that sigh and fall from your Table ?* And to undervalue the other, (*t*) *Shall she* [a Maiden] *lie in the Arms of such an enervate*

(*q*) *Luke* 16. 21.

(*q*) *Luke* 16. 23.

(*s*) The Roving Husband Reclaim'd, page 32. line 16.

(*t*) The Amorous Miser, page 12. line 24.

enervate Cripple ? She had better lie in Abraham's *Bosom.*

This is the Interpretation of our *Saviour's* Words ; and since *it is enough for the disciple that he is as his master,* we may expect to find more of this *Language*; and indeed it is remarkable that not one *Apostle* scapes them.

To begin with St. *Paul.* He argues (*t*) very seriously. *What shall we say then ? Shall we continue in sin that grace may abound ? God forbid ! How shall we that are dead unto sin live any longer therein ?* The *Language* of the (*u*) *Stage* is thus: *Such a Kindness would encourage us to sin again.* [Ans.] *And if it should!* ―― [Reply.] *'Twould give Occasion for the pleasing Exercise of Mercy.* [Ans.] *Right ! And so we act the part of Heaven and Earth together, and tast of both their Pleasures.* Here *Sin* is commended, and the *Mercy* of *God* is droll'd upon, being made an Occasion of our Security. It is the Pleasure of Men, in the *Play-House Language,* not to be Religious, but to run on in *Sin,* after Oaths and Vows to the contrary ; and the Pleasure of *God* to pardon such presumptuous Sinners.

St. Paul

(*t*) Rom. 6. 1, 2.

(*u*) The Mistake, page 44. line 15.

94

The Scriptures burlesqu'd

St. *Paul* (*x*) is very warm against such as slandered the *Apostles*, that they *walked according to the flesh*, and saith, *For though we walk in the flesh, we do not war after the flesh.* An *Actor* saith upon the *Stage*, (*y*) *I am Flesh as well as Spirit, and my Body must have some Conversation* [spoken of Whoring] *as well as my Soul.*

St. *Paul* (*z*) saith, *Every creature of God is good, and nothing to be refused, if it be received with thanksgiving. For it is sanctified by the word of God, and by prayer.* The *Play-House* expounds it thus, (*a*) *Every Creature of God is good. Every thing is good in its Kind, Cards are harmless Bits of Paper; Dice insipid Bones, and Women were made for Men.*

The *Apostle* tells us also (*b*) that *Marriage is honourable among all men, and the bed undefiled, but whoremongers and adulterers God will judge:* And that (*c*) *Marriage* was appointed by *God*, as a Means *to avoid Fornication*. For this Reason, the *Actors* render it as dishonourable as they can; complain of *God's* Providence in this Particular, expose it by all the ridiculous Similitudes, and render it the unhappiest State in the World

(*x*) 2 Cor. 10. 2, 3, 4, 5.

(*y*) Gibraltar, Sheet E. page 36. line 28.

(*z*) 1 Tim. 4. 4

(*a*) The Basset Table, page 48. line 17.

(*b*) Hebrews 13. 4.

(*c*) 1 Cor. 7. 2, 9.

World. I have not said half which may be obſerved from (*d*) the Quotations in the Margin, which would fill ſeveral Pages upon Occaſion. In ſhort, *Marriage* is a Means to prevent *Whoring*, for which Reaſon they ſo exclaim againſt it : And ſince *God* calls it Honourable, therefore they endeavour to render it *Contemptible: Whores* in the *Scripture* are accounted (*e*) abominable; but according to (*f*) the *Play-Houſe Language*, they ſhould expect greater Privileges than *Married Women*.

(*d*) An Act at Oxford, page 14. line 12. p 20. l 11. p 54. l 4. Fortune in her Wits, page 50. line penult. Gibraltar, page 3. line 3. Sheet E p 38. l 6. p 58. l 33. Hampſtead Heath, page 16. line 29. p 22. l 22. Love at firſt Sight, page 1. line 1. p 6. l 33. p 49. l 4. Love the Leveller, page 17. line 19. The Careleſs Husband, page 18. line 7 and 33. p 20. l 30. p 52. l 23. The Cares of Love, page 3. line 24. p 48. l 5 and 13. The Confederacy, page 25. line 33, to the End; and p 26, from line 1, to line 33. The Britiſh Enchanters, page 28. line 7. The Gameſter, Epilogue, line 5. The Lawyer's Fortune, page 63. line 17. The Portſmouth Heireſs, page 9. line 30. p 31. l 5. p ult. l 22.

(*e*) Deut. 23. 17, 18.

(*f*) The Careleſs Husband, page 2. line 37. p 4. l 3.

As for their Comment on (*g*) St. *James*, I have (*h*) already infiſted on it, and it needs no Repetition.

(*g*) Chap. 4.
(*h*) Page 40.

St. *Peter* tells us alſo of the *Devil* (*i*) *that he goeth about ſeeking whom he may devour*; This in the *Play-Houſe* is (*k*) applied to an *Actor*, with very little Alteration, and ſerves for a *profane* Jeſt, tho' I doubt there is too much Truth in it.

(*i*) 1 Peter 5. 8.
(*k*) The Biter, page 52. line 10.

St. *John*

(*l*) 1 *John* 1. 8.
(*m*) The Fair Example, pa. 64, line 33.

St. *John* also (*l*) informs us, that *If we say we have no sin, we deceive our selves, and the truth is not in us.* In a late (*m*) *Comedy, Symons* being catechiz'd, *What Sins he had been guilty of which had drawn a Judgment upon him,* makes this Answer, *None*, Sir, *none, I never committed any Sin in my Life*; and after Examination having own'd himself guilty of *Cheating, Lying, Betraying a Trust,* and *Aspersing his Neighbour,* he was again ask'd (*n*) *Are these*

(*n*) Page 65, line 11.

no Sins ? To which he readily answers, *Why no! I have been told, that nothing is a Sin but Swearing and Sabbath-Breaking.* Whether the *Actors* are guilty of the latter of these Crimes, I shall not determine, but I am sure they are scandalously guilty of the former. Besides, what Wit our *English Poets* shew in such Expressions as these, I cannot imagine; since a wiser Man than them

(*o*) *Prov.* 14. 9.

hath plainly told us, that (*o*) they are *Fools* who thus *make a mock at sin.*

(*p*) Verse 6.

St. *Jude* tells us (*p*) that *as for the Angels which kept not their first estate, but left their own habitation, God reserved them under chains of darkness to the judgment of the great day:* He turn'd them into *Devils,* In a late *Comedy*

a

a (r) fine *Lady* declares her *Chaſtity*, (r) The Portſmouth Heireſs, *page* 11. *line* 6. that *She did not deal altogether ſo much in the Fleſh*; to which the profane Spark, endeavouring to debauch her, makes this Anſwer; *Nay, now thou talk'ſt like a fallen Angel, repining at the Loſs of Paradiſe.* A pretty Compliment to his Miſtreſs, to compare her to the *Devil!* A fine Deſcription of *Paradiſe,* to reſemble it to a *Whoring Intriegue!* And an excellent Occaſion to burleſque the *Scriptures!*

From hardneſs of Heart and contempt of thy Word and Commandment, Good Lord deliver us.

These *Pills* are very good Preparatives to the following Deſign, and when the *Stage-Patients* can ſwallow them, the next thing is to ridicule *Devotion* in general. They firſt expoſe the Principles of *Revealed,* and then of *Natural Religion.* Some of the *Heathens* oppoſed *Plays,* as things of pernicious Conſequence; and therefore the *Players* think their Cauſe will not do well, until they can ſink *Chriſtianity* a Degree below *Paganiſm*; and then Men will be *Lovers of Pleaſure more*

H   *than*

98   *Religion undermin'd*

(s) An Act at Oxford, page 17. line 26. Gibraltar. *Sheet* E page 38. line 1. Hampstead Heath, *page* 20. *line* 1. Love at first Sight, *page* 24. *line* 23. P 49. *in fine.* Squire Trelooby, *Prologue,* *line* 3. The Basset Table, *page* 9. *line* 15. p 46. l 7. The Lawyer's Fortune, *page* 45. Signature G 3 line 8.

than *Lovers* of God. They strive to stifle *Conscience,* destroy all Notions of God and *Judgment, Heaven* and *Hell, Good* and *Evil,* and banish whatsoever hath a Tendency to grave and serious Thoughts. Many (s) Instances of this Nature may be produced, fitter for the Hands of a *Common Hangman* than the *Publick View;* and therefore I must beg the Reader's Pardon for producing some, that he may the better guess at the rest.

Fortune in her Wits, *p.* 34. *l.* 27.

What? Is the Sot grown Religious? Sirrah, I shall be ashamed of you, and disown you, if I find any more of these Conscientious Qualms.

The Fair Example, *p.* 10. *l.* 5.

What an unpolished thing was I before? On a Sunday in the Afternoon, not a Card, not a Dice, no Diversion; and for the Evening, that, Forsooth, must be spent in Roasting Apples, a long Chapter, &c.

The Inference from hence, naturally follows, That since *Religion* is a scandalous

lous **Thing**, a dull, heavy Employment, and in short, a Cheat; therefore we must down with it, let the *Professors* be of what *Perswasion* soever. *The Stage Beaux toss'd in a Blanket* hath a *Prologue* exactly calculated for this Purpose from the Beginning to the End; wherein he scourgeth in their Turns, all Pretenders to *Religion*, *Zeal* and *Honesty*, but particularly vents his Spleen against all *Preachers*, let them belong either to the *Church* or *Dissenters*; and for this Purpose, the *Speaker* is dress'd in a ridiculous Habit, one half like a *Minister* of the *Church* of *England*, and the other half like a *Dissenting Teacher*, and sometimes points to one Side, sometimes to the other, representing both as the greatest Villains in Nature. Indeed the *Title Page* tells us that the *Prologue* is against *Occasional Conformity*; but if it did not, no one who reads the *Prologue* could believe it, unless in this Sence; They would have Men totally abstain from both, and therefore reflect on such as on any Occasion resort to either.

But the *Church of England* seems to be the chief Mark at which they aim, and therefore they frequently make the

(*t*) Gibraltar, Sheet E page 36. line 34. The Portsmouth Heiress page 10. line 24. p 49. l 13.

Expressions in the sacred Office of (*t*) Baptism, the Subject of their Pastime. Nay, they who declare, that they *renounce all Women, except one, as heartily as ever they renounced the Devil,* explain their meaning in other Places of the same *Play,* lest they should be supposed really to renounce the *Devil*;

(*u*) Gibraltar, page 3. l. 3.
(*x*) Gibraltar, Sheet E page 38. line 7.

That (*u*) *none but Madmen are in love with one particular Object,* and that (*x*) *Marriage and Constancy is a purchasing of long Repentance with the Expence of Liberty.* This is the same in Effect, as if they had said, 'Tis true, in their *Baptismal Vow* they renounced the *Devil,* but it was never done heartily; at best, it was a mad Trick,

(*y*) An Act at Oxford, *page* 11. line ult. p 17. l 27.
Hampstead Heath, *page* 15. line 13.
(*z*) The Careless Husband, *page* 5. line 9.
(*a*) The Careless Husband, *page* 6. line 12.
(*b*) The Roving Husband Reclaim'd, *page* 33. line 16.

it might have cost them their Liberty, and they are sorry for it ever since.

Neither is it one particular Office, but all who frequent the *Church,* especially on Week-Days, *Plays* being then acted, are (*y*) Censur'd and Ridicul'd. In one *Comedy* (*z*) a *Lady* saith, *She is going to Church*; From whence this Observation is (*a*) afterward made, *I know, Women of your Principles have more Pride than those who have no Principles at all.* In (*b*) another, there is this Expression; *The Church! I scorn your Words, Sir, I deal in no such Cattle,*

tle, I want no Luck in Horse Flesh.
To which this Answer is return'd;
*I like your Cause the better, for not
having to do with the Church.*

To conclude this *Chapter,* I shall
only observe, That the Design of the
Play-House is to promote *Atheism* in
the World. For this Purpose they
speak their Minds freely on some Occasions. Thus an *Actor* tells us (*c*)
his own Religion. *I seldom trouble the
Gods, except it be to swear by them;*
and that (*d*) *the Wits indeed were A-
theists in old Times, and they were brave
Examples,* for Men to follow; with
other (*e*) Sentences to the same Purpose.

(c) Love the
Leveller, *page
5. line 6.*
(d) Love at
first sight, *page
9. line 3.*
(e) The
Amorous Mi-
ser, *page 9.
line 22.* The
Loyal Subject,
*page 44. line
18.*

But if they cannot prevail to make
Men *Atheists,* they have another Card
to play, which is to make them *Hypocrites.* Either *Method* may ruin their
Souls, and gratify the *Devil.* 'Tis
true indeed, sometimes the *Stage* ex-
claims against *Hypocrites;* but then
they only mean such as endeavour to
suppress *Profaneness* and *Debauchery,* or
such as write against, or would reform the *Play-House.* These are horrid
and dreadful Evils in their Opinion. But
a bare Shew of *Religion,* when the Heart
is set on other Things is among them
rather

rather esteem'd as a *Virtue.* In the *Portsmouth Heiress,* Captain *Rainer* is the principal Man of *Figure* throughout the whole *Play,* the *Drama* saith, he is *free and well bred;* and in the End he Marries, *L' Bell,* the principal Woman, and great Fortune, from whence the *Play* took its Name, and (f) *Page* 5. therefore what (*f*) he saith is the line penult. more material, which I shall set down at large.

In the old Remains of *Truth, Im-probity* and *Hypocrisy* are painted the darling *Principles* of the *Fortunate.* A *dissembled Virtue,* like a *dissembled Pas-sion,* hath commonly the best *Effect.* Gravity and affected Zeal grow farther in the Eye of the World than Sincerity and plain Dealing; and were I to rong a Man in his Estate, or a Woman in her Honour, it should be still under the Hy-pocritical Cant of Devotion. To this it is answer'd; A pretty Religion you profess, truly! And he immediately replies, Religion! Ay, there's another Topick now! Religion and Reformati-on! Prithee what hath Religion to do with a Man of Figure? Conscience re-sides among poor Rogues; Men of Qua-lity are above it.

The

The *Greek Tragedians* speak honou-
rably of their *Gods*, which was com-
mendable in them, because they knew
no other; they endeavour to instil
into their *Hearers* the Notions of *Natural Religion:* And therefore, I wish
our *Poets* would imitate these *Heathens;* since the Attempts for their
Reformation cannot prevail upon them
to write like *Christians.*

CHAP.

CHAP. V.

The Doctrines of Christianity misapplied by the Stage.

(*a*) Gibraltar, page 5. line 1. Love the Leveller, page 5. line 6. Squire Treloooby, page 20. line 1 and antepenult. p 21. l 10. The Mistake, page 57. Signature I line 9.

(*b*) Love at first Sight, page 49. line 11. The Female Wits, page 61. line 12. The Mistake, page 28. line 25.

(*c*) Fortune in her Wits, page 27, line 30. Gibraltar, Sheet F. page 44, line 30 and 36. The Roving Husband, reclaim'd, page 8, line 21.

IT cannot be supposed that they who thus endeavour to undermine *Religion*, pervert and burlesque the *Scriptures*, and turn the most serious Parts of them into *profane Jests*, will behave themselves in a Different Manner, when they speak of those Truths which we are taught thereby. If the *Poets* are willing to be merry in their *Comedies*, let them take other Subjects for the Matter of their Jests. *Religion* and the *Scriptures* require our serious Thoughts. It is ill *Jesting* with (*a*) *God*, (*b*) *Death*, (*c*) and the *Devil*. *God* will not be mock'd, *Death* mocks all Men, and the *Devil* alone is gratified by such Diversions. However, such Expressions as these must be spoken on the *Stage*, to make the Hearers laugh, and the Subject ridiculous. It would certainly be a greater Reputation to the *Poet*, in the Choice of his Words, to avoid all such Sayings

as

as bring *Religion* into Contempt, and cause the *Actors* to speak worse than *Heathens.* But since they scruple no *Blasphemy*, rather than loose a *Fancy*, and since they complain, that [*d*] the Denying them this *Liberty*, will *Rob them of all their Life and Pertness*; I hope, they will remember, that *It is ill Jesting with Serious Things.* It will leave an ill Impression on the Minds of the *Hearers* - And for such *idle Words*, there must be a serious *account on the day of judgment.* If they cannot write, but they must write *profanely*, they had much better not write at all. If they cannot bear a *due Correction*, they justly deserve a *total Suppression.* And it is high Time to abolish the *Play-Houses*, since they *profane the Name of God*, and *expose Religion* in so publick a Manner.

(d) The Portsmouth Heiress. *Preface line 4.*

The Sum of the *Christian Religion*, contain'd in the *Holy Scriptures*, are usually reduced to two Heads, namely, *Doctrine* and *Precept*; The *Precepts* are either *positive*, commanding *Virtue*, or *negative*, forbidding *Vice.* If then the *Stage* misapplies the *Doctrines of Christianity*, if it *exposes Virtue*, and if it *encourages Vice*; then it is evident, that

that it directly exposes the whole Design of the *Scripture* and the *Christian Religion*.

For a Proof, that the *Doctrines of Christianity are misapplied by the Stage*, I shall only produce some *Quotations*, and leave them to the Consideration of the *Reader*.

First, The Notion of *Grace* is strangely misapplied. In [e] one *Comedy*, the utmost Perfection thereof is lodg'd in an *affected, amorous, old Widow*. In [f] another. *Chastity* is expos'd as a Want of *Grace*. In [g] another *Play*, *Phædra* reads her Husband a *Lesson* of Obedience to her, and gives him several Directions for this Purpose, and then concludes thus ; *Be sure, remember what hath been said, and may* Juno *give you Grace to apply it aright*. Here *Preaching* is ridicul'd, the *Honour* due to *God* given to a *Pagan Deity*, and the Notion of *Grace* expos'd ; so that there is a triple Discharge against *Religion* in a single Sentence.

Secondly, The Doctrine of *Predestination* is misapplied. [h] *This*, saith an Actor, *is the very Predestination of good Fortune* ; spoken of an accidental Meeting on the *Stage*. In the *Articles*
of

[e] The Biter, *page* 5. *line* 23.
[f] The Cares of Love, *page* 10, *line* 34.
[g] Solon, *page* 26. *line* 31.

[h] The Biter, *page* 7. *line* 30.

of the *Church of England*, *Predestina-*
tion is [i] defcrib'd as an Act of *God's*
Providence, and it ought not therefore to be afcrib'd to any other. [k]
———*Sed te* ———— *Nos facimus, Fortuna,*
Deam, cæloq; locamus. ——But now, *For-*
tune is a *Goddefs*, fhe is plac'd in *Heav'n*,
and the Word *Predestination* is applied
to the paltry Concerns of the *Stage.*

    Thirdly, The Doctrine of *God's Pro-*
vidence is as ftrangely mifapplied. In
[l] one *Play*, an *Actor* fpeaking of an
Intreague for *Adultery*, and perfwa-
ding the Husband with a Bribe to confent, makes this Inference; *See, there's*
a Providence in it, which nothing can
refist. Another [m] alfo fpeaking of
Lust in a marrried Woman, to commit *Adultery*, foftens it with the Name
of *Love*, and faith, *He that creates*
Love, if it was fo bad a thing, no doubt
he would prevent it. Here *God* is
blam'd for our Mifcarriages, and the
Fault laid on him but not on our
felves. When our firft Parents finn'd,
Adam laid the Blame upon *Eve*, and
Eve upon the *Devil*, and neither of
them durft lay the Blame upon *God*:
But here it is remarkable, That tho'
each of thefe did *wickedly*, yet in this
Refpect

[i] *Article* 17.

[k] *Juvenal,* Satyr 10. ver. penult.

[l] Love the Leveller, page 8. line 12.

[m] The Roving Husband Reclaim'd, page 19. line penult.

Respect, our present *Stage* exceeds them

[n] The Ro- all. Nay, The same *Comedy* in [n]
ving Husband another place, makes *God* the *Author*
Reclaim'd,
page 59. line 7. of our *Transgressions*, and speaks in the
Case of *Adultery*:

> *Ne'er think 'tis a Sin ; of a Truth I do*
> *   know,*
> *'Tis the Will of the Fates, and they will*
> *   have it so.*

[o] The Mi- In [o] another *Comedy*, *Sin* is ex-
stake, page 44. cus'd, because it gives *Occasion for the*
line 1 &c.
pleasing Exercise of Mercy; and thus they
speak of heinous *Offences*, as if they
had no Notion of *Good and Evil*,
But then, to make a farther Jest of
this Matter, they apply the Notion of
of *Sin* to such things, as are trifling
[p] The Baf- and insignificant. An *Actor* [p] speak-
set Table, page ing to some who laugh at a ridiculous
38. line ult.
[q] Love's, *Letter* saith, *I warrant Heaven will*
Contrivance, *punish you all* : And another [q] cries
printed 1703.
page 55. line 1. out in a Passion. *Is it not an horrible*
thing ; a thing that cries to Heaven for
Vengeance, that it should be said publick-
ly, The Form of an Hat ? I affirm they
should say, The Figure of an Hat, and
not The Form.   Thus trifling Matters
must be gross *Sins*, and gross *Sins*
must be nothing at all.   To

To this I shall only add, That they represent themselves and others as absolutely perfect, and guilty of no *Sin* at all. One [*r*] speaks of himself, that *he never committed any Sin in his Life,* and puts it off with a Jest, rather to be lamented than laugh'd at. And [*s*] another speaks of his *Mistress.*

[*r*] The Fair Example, page 64, line 33.

[*s*] The British Enchanters, page 15, line 13.

The faultless Form no secret Stains
  disgrace,
A Beauteous Mind, unblemish'd as her
  Face.
Not Painted and Adorn'd to varnish Sin;
Without, all Goodness; all Divine within.
By Truth maintaining what by Love she
  got,
A Heaven without a Cloud, a Sun without
  a Spot,

The *Scriptures* tell us, That [*t*] there should be some, *who privily bring in damnable heresies, and bring upon themselves swift destruction; and that many shall follow their own pernicious ways, by reason of whom the way of truth shall be evil spoken of.* We ought therefore to be very cautious in admitting such *Rhetorick* and *Diversion,* since we know not the Consequence

[*t*] 2 Pet. 2. 1, 2.

quence thereof ; and have great Reason to joyn with the *Church* in this Petition :

　　From all false Doctrine, Heresy and Schism, Good Lord Deliver us.

CHAP.

CHAP VI.

Virtue expos'd by the Stage

FROM the *Doctrines* taught upon the *Stage*, I shall proceed to their *Precepts* ; and as I have already spoken of their *Swearing, Cursing, Blasphemy*, and their undermining of *Religion* ; so I shall take no farther Notice of the *Duties* and *Sins*, which refer immediately to *God*, but only of such, as relate to our *selves* and our *Neighbours*.

Tho' the *Heathens* were led only by the Light of Nature ; yet both the *Greeks* and *Latins* wrote very excellently upon *Moral* Subjects. When *God* at first revealed his Will, he gave us the *Ten Commandments* which is called *The Morral Law*, and afterward farther Exhortations which were agreeable thereto. When our *Saviour* was upon the Earth, he charg'd us, saying, (a) *Think not, that I am come to destroy the law and the prophets ; I am not come to destroy, but to fulfil.* The *Apostles* treat on such *Topicks*, as excellently as the *Prophets* ; and therefore the Precepts of *Morality* are what *Heathens*,

(a) Math 5. 17.

Heathens, Jews, Turks, and *Christians*
of all Perswasions, are fully agreed in.
But the *Language* of the *Play-Houses,*
being Peculiar from all the World besides, may be seen in these following
Particulars.

First, They represent *Virtue* as
nothing, but an Appearance only. He
is *Virtuous,* in the *Play-House Language,*
who hath a good Reputation; and he
is *Vicious,* who is so unfortunate, as to
expose himself to Censure. He who
is as *Vicious* as the worst, let him keep
it private, and in their Opinion he is
as *Virtuous* as the best. In *(b)* one
Play, an *Actor* speaking of *Adultery,*
saith, *We will be both virtuous, that is,
we will be secret, and the World shall
never know the contrary.* In another
(c) there is much to the same Purpose spoken on the same Subject. *Will
these Consciencious Qualms be never reconciled to Love?* [that is Adultery.
Answer] *And if it should be known.*
[Reply] *'Twould prove a Sin. But if it
should not then you are innocent and virtuous.* [Answer] *Then Virtue is nothing
but a Name.* [Reply] *What else? She
is innocent, who is reputed such, and
lewd whom every Body believes to be so.*

(b) An Act
at Oxford, pa.
25, line 24.
Hampstead
Heath, page
29, line 3.

(c) Love at
first Sight, pa.
39, line 16.

In

In a third there is alſo (*d*) this Ex-
preſſion. *What is a Crime to the Wicked,
may not be ſo to the Godly. If you
guard well the Appearance, half the
Duty of Religion is preſerv'd, and you
avoid the Scandal. Now the Crime as
to Men is none, if not known, and in
many reputed Crimes, the Scandal is all
the Offence, as particularly, in a private
Amour, where there is no Injury. If ſuch
Communications do not corrupt good
Manners,* and ſuch *Arguments* do not
directly tend to confound all Notions
of *Virtue* and *Vice*, I know not what
doth. Beſides, We are told, that (*e*)
the *Pleaſure of Virtue is not ſo much
in the Thing, as in the Reputation
of having it*; and (*f*) That *there is
nothing in that Religion, which debars
a Man of his Pleaſure.* 'Tis well
known that the *Heathens* taught different *Morals,* and declared, that Man's
chief Happineſs in this Life, conſiſted
in the Practice of *Virtue.* The *Prophet Iſaiah* (*g*) pronounceth an heavy
*Woe againſt them, that do but call evil
good, and good evil*; *that put darkneſs
for light, and light for darkneſs*; *that
put bitter for ſweet, and ſweet for bitter.*
The *Actors* render themſelves liable to

(*d*) The Stage Beaux toſs'd in a Blanket, *page* 57. *line* 24.

(*e*) The Careleſs Husband, *page* 24 *line* antepenult.

(*f*) The Portſmouth Heireſs, *page* 6. *line* 21.

(*g*) *Chap.* 5 20.

this

this *Wo.* They afcribe the Name of *Virtue* to *Vice. Winking at the Adultery* of an Husband, is ftiled (*h*) *the moſt convenient piece of Virtue, that ever a Wife was Miſtreſs of.* In (*i*) one *Play*, a notorious *Whore* is publickly convicted before a Mock *Juſtice of the Peace*, who makes this Apology for the Fact : *She hath committed a little Country Folly, as ſhe privately confeſſeth. What's that ! It may ſtand in Rank with what they call Virtue here.* I hope there will be no Danger in expoſing the Poiſon, and therefore I ſhall add ſome other Quotations.

(*h*) The Careleſs Husband, page 6. line 33.

(*i*) The Northern Laſs, page 46. line antepenult.

(*k*) *Virtue ! Can you feed upon it ?*

(*l*) *Some Virtuous Devil.*

(*m*) *Virtue ! with a Pox to't.*

(*n*) *To loſe Money, and long of this Virtue [with an Oath] I wonder how this Virtue crept into my Houſe ; I am ſure I never gave it any Encouragement.*

(*o*) *What good hath your Virtue done you ?*

(*p*) *Virtues in a Wife, are good for nothing, but to make her Proud, and*

(*k*) Fortune in her Wits, page 50. line 3.

(*l*) Love at firſt Sight. page 8. line 17.

(*m*) Love the Leveller, page 22. line 6.

(*n*) Love the Leveller, page 22. line 12.

(*o*) The Careleſs Husband, page 6. line 4.

(*p*) The Careleſs Husband, page 19. line 9.

put

put the World in mind of her Husband's Faults.

(q) *I think, as the World goes, they may be proud of marrying their Daughter into a Virtuous Family.* To this it is answer'd, with an Oath: *Vertue is not the Case*; and when it was reply'd, *Where she may have a good Example before her Eyes,* this Expression was farther exposed by drolling upon the Name of *God.*

(q) The Confederacy, page 32. line 35.

The Last Expressions which I shall mention, are spoken by a *Gentleman* (r) of *good Breeding,* and who makes an honourable *Exit* by marrying the great Fortune in the *Play.* I must confess, his Sentences are remarkable. (s) *Give me as much Pleasure, I say, as my Constitution requires; as much Wit and Sincerity as will qualify me for Company; and just as much Morality as will secure me from the Talons of the Law, and let Fortune take her Choice.* And (t) a little after, *Urge your Virtue to a Courtier, and he'll receive you as a young Lord do's a begging Relation. Urge your Virtue to a Lawyer, and you may plead your Cause your self. Urge your Virtue to*

(r) The Portsmouth Heiress, Rainer *in the Drama.*

(s) Page 5. line 13.

(t) Page 5. line 23.

I 2

a *Woman, and she'll enquire into your E-
state. In short, Virtue is like a Man's
Coat of Arms, of no Value to any but
himself, and he that depends to rise by
that one Quality alone, may e'en be reduced to starve with his Mistress.* To
this it is answer'd; *Excellent Satyr
this! Prithee where hast thou learnt it?*
And he immediately replys; *From the
old Remains of Truth, where Improbity
and Hypocrisy are painted, the darling
Principles of the Fortunate,*

Thus the *Old Remains of Truth* are
strangely misrepresented by the *Stage*,
to condemn all *Morality*, and encourage
Hypocrisy. Accordingly, in (*u*) another
Comedy, an *Antient Philosopher* speaks
in very different *Language* from his
real Character; and concludes the *Play*
with an Instruction to the Audience
from his own Example, *viz.*

(*t*) Solon,
page 1 lit. line
antepenult.

Unpolish'd Morals I'll no longer prize.

Besides the Arguments mentioned in
Scripture, there are two other Motives
to *Virtue*, viz. *Honour* and *Conscience*.
Mr. *Congreve* hath given these their
joynt Character in a (*x*) former *Comedy*,
That *Honour is a publick Enemy, and*
Con-

(*x*) Love for
Love, printed
1704, being the
4th Edition.
page 43, line 32

Conscience a domestick Thief; and our
late *Poets* follow this great Example of
Reformation. One (*y*) speaks of *Ho-*
nour; *What is Honour? A noisy No-*
thing, a stalking Shade ; *when 'tis lost,*
no one finds it, and Heaven be prais'd,
there's not many look after it now.
When they have it, 'tis us'd like their
Cloaths, fond of it at first, till they find
something they like better, and then 'tis
gone with a Fadding. Another speaks
of *Conscience,* (*z*) That *it resides among*
poor Rogues, and Men of Dignity are a-
bove it; and in another Place, (*a*) *Con-*
science, they say, has a Sting, but hath
not Love a greater ? O yes, Villains can
suffer Shame and live after it, but
Lovers cannot brook Despair.

Beside the general Discouragement
which the *Stage* gives to *Virtue*, it will
not, I hope, be improper to mention
in some particular Instances, how they
represent those *Virtues* which relate to
our selves.

First, The *Stage* exposeth *Chastity,*
sometimes as (*b*) an *Impossibility*; sometimes as (*c*) a bare *Fancy*; and sometimes as (*d*) a Want of *Grace.* The

(*y*) The Ro-
ving Husband
Reclaim'd,
page 32. line
22.

(*z*) The
Portsmouth
Heiress, page
6. line 14.
(*a*) Page 25.
line 3.

(*b*) As you
find it, print-
ed 1703, page
33. line 30.
(*c*) The Care-
less Husband,
page 34. line
antepenult.

(*d*) The Cares of Love, *page* 10. *line* 34.

late

(e) The Roaring Husband, reclaim'd, page 32, line 22.

(f) The Cares of Love, page 10, line 33.

late (*e*) Expression in general concerning *Honour*, was particularly meant of this *Virtue*. In one (*f*) *Comedy*, *Lucinda* saith, *I am called by the Name of her who was an Example of Chastity*. To this, it is answer'd; *But I hope you have more Grace than to let it go farther than your Name.* Nay, they represent it as the (*) *Sin of Ingratitude. Rather than be tax'd with such a Sin* [saith an *Actor*] *she'll be yours for nothing, at least for no Money.*

Secondly, The *Stage exposeth Preparation for Death*, and another World, which ought to be the proper Business of our whole Life.

(g) The Female Wits, page 61, line 12.

(h) Love at first Sight, page 49, line 11. The Mistake, page 28, line 25.

(*g*) *My Lady dying! I am not yet prepar'd to bear her Company. I'll e'en shift for one. I would not willingly leave this wicked World, before I have tasted a little more on't.* Other (*h*) Quotations might be added, but I think one is sufficient.

(i) Love at first Sight, page 43, line 5.

Thirdly, *Fasting* is *misapplied.* (*i*) A Man almost Drunk, when he can have no more Wine brought him, is represented as *Fasting for the Sins of the Day.*

(k) The Careless Husband, page 28, line 11.

Fourthly, Another speaks of *Humility* (*k*) *What have you to do with it? Will*
                                        you

you never have enough of it? If *Humility* is a Fault, the *Poets* and *Actors* are seldom guilty, and therefore may I confess more boldly expose it.

Lastly, They *expose Modesty* and call it (*l*) a *sickly sneaking Virtue.*

I shall now conclude this Chapter with their Notions of such *Virtues* as relate to our Neighbours.

First, They *rail at Honesty,* (*m*) in general, *They'd make us honest, that's they'd make us Fools.* They rail more particularly at (*n*) honest Love. *What! turn'd Chymist in Love? Extracting Patience from the meer Necessity of a Woman's Inconstancy!* [with an Oath] *That a Man of Sence should be thus Ass rid and not feel himself gall'd! wilt thou never be wise.*

Secondly, They *expose Obedience to Parents,* especially in the the Case of *Love.* This is a fine Lesson for young Ladies that frequent them. *If* (*o*) *he was my Father* [saith one] *I should take a great Pleasure to plague him.* Another (*p*) faith, *My Heart begins to fail me* ; and asks this Question, *shall I resist my Father?* To this it is answered, *When he resists Nature. Are you to be a Gosling all your Life? Are you not of Age to*

(*l*) Solon, Epilogue, page 2. line 10.

(*m*) The Stage Beaux toss'd in a Blanket, Prologue, page 2. line 15.
(*n*) The Portsmouth Heiress, page 47. line 9.

(*o*) The Quacks, page 5. line 1.
(*p*) The Quacks, page 6. line 19.

I 4   *be*

be married? And doth he think you are made of Marble? If the Difposal of Children in Marriage is the great Concern of Parents, and that upon which their own Comfort, the Comfort of their Children and the Honour of their Family depends, and if they would have them dutiful in this Refpect, they ought to keep them from the *Play-Houfe.*

By this we may obferve how excellently the *Stage* promotes *Virtue*, and endeavours to reclaim the Age. Let every Man live as they pleafe, be guilty of *Whoring*, be *Drunk*, *Impudent*, and *Shamelefs*, and never mind either *Death* or *Judgment*; then the *Actors* will thrive, their *Houfes* will be full, and (*which God forbid*) they will effect their intended *Reformation.*

CHAP.

CHAP. VII.

Vice encouraged by the Stage.

TO prove that the *Stage encourageth Vice*, and is also in this respect as equally guilty as in the other, I shall first produce some general Quotations to this Purpose, and leave them to the Consideration of the Reader.

(*a*) "We ought to sin seasona-
"bly, to drink in *Spain*, and whore in
"*London*, where the Wenches are good
"and cheap, and the Tax free. *(a) Gibraltar, page 6. line 14.*

(*b*) "Vice, by the Dexterity of
"of our Council, is made the Suppor-
"ter of Religion and the Laws. *(b) Gibraltar, page 6. line 21.*

(*c*) "For a Look and a Chink of
"this [*Mony*] who now a Days would
"not be a Sinner? *(c) Gibraltar, page 22. line 25.*

(*d*) "I hate to sin like a Porter,
"that's damnable; but to sin in State,
"and like a Gentleman, I hope, is
"venial. *(d) Love at first Sight, page 14. line 16.*

(*e*) "Vice

(e) Love at
first Sight,
page 30. line
23.

(e) "Vice when dress'd by him
" [*an Actor*] hath Charms about her.

(f) The
Portsmouth
Heiress, page
7. line 8:
spoken by the
Well bred Gen-
tleman.

(f) "Thou art fond of Vice for the
" sake of the Scandal. [*Answer*] Ay,
" Ay, you may give it what Names you
" please; but the dear Felicity of Life
" is concealed under these hideous Ti-
" tles [*by calling it Vice &c.*] like a
" good Face under a frightful Vizor:
" And as there is no Preferment to
" be had without Interest; so there is
" no Pleasure to be had without Scan-
' dal.

But to be more particular. To this
End they apply the *Act of Parliament*
pass'd in the late Reign for *Toleration* of
the *Protestant Dissenters*. If a Man can
commit a *Sin* without a scruple, they
say he hath his *Liberty* by Law, and may
go on. Thus *Liberty of Conscience* is
render'd as a *Liberty* to act without any
Conscience at all. This is a bold Reflection upon the *Legislative Power*, and if
this *Liberty* is not restrained, it may
prove of pernicious Consequence. This

(g) Love's
Contrivance,
printed 1703.
page 17. line
antepenult.

Act of Parliament is particularly applied
to encourage *Adultery*. *Women* (g) cannot please long (saith an Actor) *if they*
                                        affect

affect an arbitrary sway [to keep their Husbands to themselves] and the Reason he gives is, because there is *Liberty of Conscience.* Another also *(h)* speaks more fully to the Purpose. *Every Man after his own Fancy, I say you are for a Whore, I am for a Bottle. As long as there is Liberty of Conscience abroad, Why should not every Man be damn'd in his own Way?* These are their *Reports* upon the *Statutes* of this *Realm.* Blessed be *God,* we have good Laws lately made for the suppressing of *Immorality* and *Profaneness.* These *Laws* have been also put in Execution. Some of the *Players* have also felt the Smart of them; and therefore they are Angry, and cannot forbear shewing their Resentments against the *Law-Makers,* and rendering them ridiculous. *I,* saith one, *will* [*i*] *petition the House of Commons to prove me a Cuckold, and be Divors'd by Act of Parliament.* I wish they would *petition* for their farther Regulation, or others would *Petition* for their Total Suppression, and hope that either the one or other would be soon granted. The *Parliament* made an *Act* in the late Reign, against *profane Swearing and Cursing.*

(h) Gibraltar, *Sheet E* page 39. line 25.

(i) Hamstead Heath, page 48. line 21.

To

(k) Gibral=
tar, page 6.
line 18.

To this (k) one of the *Actors* refers, we pay for *Swearing*, and we pay for *Drinking*, and another infers from thence, That *thus is Vice, by the Dexterity of our Councils, made the Supporter of Religion and the Laws.* All their Efforts cannot abolish such *Acts* of *Parliament*, and therefore they thus endeavour to ridicule them.

But for a farther Encouragement of *Vice*, they represent their principal Persons, as most scandalously *vicious*, and reward them with good Wives and Fortunes at the End of the *Play*, at best they are not punished as they deserve. This was fully charg'd upon them by Mr. *Collier* in a whole Chapter on this Subject, but nothing that can be said will cause them to amend; there must be some other *Method* to reclaim them. Here I cannot but do Justice to the Author of *The Lying Lover*, who hath shewn us the ill Consequences both of *Lying* and *Drunkenness*, and (tho' there are some *Oaths* and *Curses*, from which no Modern *Play* is free, and other Expressions which I shall not justify) is the best of all those which have been lately printed. But this one ex-cepted, there is not such another In-stance.

ftance. A *Goal* is a dreadful Repre-
fentation on a S*tage*; one Inftance
is enough to terrify the whole *Pit*,
and leaves an Impreſſion when *Hell*
is thought to be a Jeft. In other *Comedies* they take other Methods, careſs
the *Atheiſts*, and reward the *Debauchees*.

In the *Comedy* of *Gibraltar* there are
no greater Perſons than *Wilmot* and
Vincent, two *Engliſh Colonels*, theſe endeavour to debauch *Leonora* and *Jacquelinda*, two *Spaniſh Ladies*, for this Purpoſe they form ſeveral Intreagues,
firft with *Guzman*, and then with
Blincarda their Governeſs, they frequently confeſs themſelves to be notorious *Whoremongers*, and are afterwards
rewarded with marrying theſe Ladies,
with two thouſand Pounds each for
their Portions.

In the *Comedy* call'd *The Confederacy*, *Dick* is a *Gameſter*, he diſowns
his *Mother*, fteals from *her*, *ſwears*
and *curſes* moft horridly, and is guilty
of many other *Vices*; he alſo marries
Corinna, a Maiden of a great Fortune,
and unexpectedly receives ten thouſand
Pounds from his *Mother* Mrs. *Amlet*:
The whole *Plot* turns upon him, ſince
the *Confederacy* in the *Play* is only a
Combi-

Combination between him and *Brass*
his Man, for all sorts of Mischief.

In *The Portsmouth Heiress* there are
three remarkable Instances of this Nature.

First, *Captain Rainer* is publickly
Debauched from the *Beginning* to the
End. At his first Entrance upon the
Stage he rails against *Religion* and *Re-formation*, and carries his Cause against
a very trivial Opposition; he pleads
for *Whoring*, and endeavours to de-bauch every Woman almost that he
meets; Acquaintance or Strangers, or
in Masks, are all alike to him. This
is a *free* and *well-bred* Gentleman,
the Principal Person in the *Play*, who
in the *End* marries *The Portsmouth
Heiress* with ten Thousand Pounds
Fortune.

Secondly, *Venture* forges *Lyes* and
Intreagues to steal a Fortune; he courts
Lucia supposing her to be *the Portsmouth Heiress*, and afterwards marries
her: However, she proves to be a
great Fortune; and thus all his Tricks
and Cheats are rewarded with Success.

Lastly, *Feignwell* forges *Lyes* of
Freemont, debauches *Maria*, then slights
her and courts another; in the *End*
he

he marries *Maria*, who had a Thousand Pound; so that these are their *Exits* after all their Roguery.

But some object, Are there not later *Plays* written, to expose the *Vices* of the Age, particularly the *Gamester*, and the *Basset Table*? And will not such contribute very much towards a *Reformation*?

To this I answer, That the chief Matter, which the *Plays* Expose, is a little *Pedantry*, *Humour*, and *Formality*, a Country Clown, or an affected Gate, which signifies nothing in Matters of *Religion*, and is in no respect inconsistent with the *Civil Government*. It may also be granted, that they sometimes expose *Covetousness*, being a *Vice* directly against their Interest, and consequently as odious to them as *Religion* and *Reformation*. But to expose *Covetousness*, before a Company of *Rakes*, *Spendthrifts*, and *Prodigals* (for such are most of those who resort to the *Play-Houses*) serves rather to sooth them in their *Vices*, and harden them in the contrary *Sin*. The *Gamester*, and the *Basset Table*, are written by the same Author, and (omitting several exceptionable Passages, are very little serviceable

serviceable to the pretended Design.
The Epilogue of the *Gamester*, speaks
against this particular *Vice*; but the
Design of the *Play*, and the Conduct
of *Valere* the *Gamester* seems rather to
infer, that *It is good to have Two
Strings to our Bow*. If we Game and
succeed therein we are provided for;
if that fails we shall pass for Gentlemen, and may marry rich Fortunes;
and tho' we break our *Oaths* and *Promises* which we made at first, yet the
Ladies will soon believe us at another
Time. For my Part I expect no good
from a *Play* were the *Devil* is invok'd
in the very first Line, and believe our
Reformation must be carried on without his Assistance. However, the Author seems sensible that there might be
good *Morality* in the *Epilogue* of the
Gamester, and therefore takes Care to
be guilty of no such Fault in the *Epilogue* of *The Basset Table*; and as in
the other *Valere* was a Loser, so in
this *The Lady Reveller* games and wins,
and is afterward married to the *Lord
Worthy*, one of the best *Reputation*. In
short, in these two *Plays* are contained
all, I think, that they can boast of
in two Years, which serves to reform

a *Vice* to which their *Hearers* may be inclin'd. From these their Champions make the great Noise of their *Reformation*, and these serve rather to amuse the World, than to amend it: And if their *Hearers* game less, which I hardly believe, it may rather be imputed to some other Cause, than to their being convinced by what was spoken on the *Stage*, in these *Comedies*.

If the *Stage* encourageth *Theft*, we can hardly expect that it will be serviceable to suppress *Gaming* ; or that they who lead others in the Way to the *Gallows*, will forewarn them of a *Sin* which hath a less Penalty. Now *Theft* is there encouraged, both by Recommendation and Example. In *The a) Metamorphosis* there is a bold Stroke. *How strangely the World is altered? Of Old, Good morrow Thief, was as kindly received, as now, your Honour. The* Spartans *aud the* Arabians *held it lawful* ; *so grew* Arabia *happy,* Sparta *Valiant.* In (*b*) *the Confederacy,* Dick *the Gamester,* readily finds the Way to his Mother's Box : And if Children and Apprentices can do the same, the *Play-House* may be full, and others will pay for it.

(a) Page 15. line 13.

(b) Page 31, 4 l, 3, line 1, &c.

K
How

However, let us suppose, for once, that they exclaim against *Gaming*; yet there is another *Vice* which they constantly recommend, I mean *Adultery* and *Whoredom*. Wherever the Word *Love* is in the *Title Page*, there the Intreagues of this Nature are represented in the Book, and drawn up even into a *Science*. A late *Comedian* made this Observation *(c)* that *Whores were Dog cheap, at* London, *and a Man might but step into the* Play-House *Passage, and pick up half a Dozen, for half a Crown.* In short, these Intreagues are the Plots upon which the *Plays* turn, both *Comedy* and *Tragedy*, and wherein their Wit is shewn; so that we may as certainly expect to find such Instances as to find both Men and Women in the *Drama.* For this Reason they frequently plead for *Adultery*, sometimes in *(d) Men,* and sometimes in *(e) Women,* and sometimes in *(f)* both, and seem wonder-

(c) Gibraltar, page 6, line 9.

(d) Love at first Sight, page 1, line ult. p 12, l. 24. The Biter, page 44, line antepenult. The Portsmouth Heiress, page 42 line 9. The Roving Husband reclaim'd, page 47. line 6. The Tender Husband, page 48, line 19. p. 49, l 4.

(e) Hampstead Heath, page 28, line 25. Perolla and Izadora, *Epilogue line* 13 *with Smut following it.* Solon, page 25, line 18. p. 48, l. 21. The Cares of Love, page 3, line 24. The Tender Husband, page 49, *line* 22.

(f) Love at first Sight, page 43, line 13 and 26. Love the Leveller, page 8, line 12. The Biter, page 44, line 21. The Conquest of Spain, page 4, line 33. The Portsmouth Heiress, page 50, *line* 17. The Roving Husband reclaim'd, page 31, *line* 17.

fully

fully pleas'd with (g) one of the married *Couple* who will wink at such *Crimes* in the other. At other Times they represent (h) *Constancy* to each other, as a scandalous *Vice* in the *Eye* of the World, they strongly (i) plead for *Whoredom,* and (k) extol the Office of a *Pimp* or *Procurer* as a Business of Weight, Merit and Authority, a civil Imployment, fit to make a Man a privy Councellor, and as no common Blessing to Mankind. Here the *Auditors* are taught in Words at Length, and not in *Figures* only, how to *debauch* the Women with whom they converse, and their Expressions are gilded over with all the *Art* and false *Rhetorick* imaginable. Here they are taught how to solicite the Lady her self, and sometimes how to intreague with the waiting Gentlewoman both by fair Words and Bribes to betray the young Mistress, or ensnare her Affections. Here they are taught how to employ even their waiting Men to intreague

(g) The Careless Husband, page 6, line 33.
(h) The Careless Husband, page 43, line 27.
(i) Gibraltar, page 3, line 3 and 34. Sheet E page 35, line 4, &c. ab large. Sheet E page 38, line 1. Sheet H pa. 49, line 27. Love at first Sight, page 3, line 4, &c. to the end. p. 4, l. 9. Love the Leveller, Epilogue line 1. The Basset Table, page 55, line 1, &c. The Fair Example, page 40, line 26. The Portsmouth Heiress, page 5, line 1. p. 50, l. 17. The Rival Brothers, page

72, line 1, &c. *with many strange Flights to this purpose.* The Careless, Husband, page 43, line 34.

(k) An act at Oxford, page 11, line 12. *repeated in* Hampstead Heath, page 13, line 26. Gibraltar, page 7, line penult. p. 10, l. 23, Sheet F p. 40, l. 13. Sheet H p. 55, l. 23. The Cares of Love, page 26, line 2.

with

with the Servants of the other Family for the same Purpose. I have read such Instances of every Particular in our Modern *Plays*, that I think it not safe to direct to them even in the Margin.

Here Men are taught *(l)* how to be *Impudent*, and take no Denial. Here are *(m) Contrivances* for Whoring represented, with *(n) Evasions* to avoid Suspicion, and a dreadful Tincture of *Smut*, sometimes in *(o) Common Discourse*, and sometimes in *(p) Verse*; were the Force of the *Musick* doubles the Mischief, and from whence our

(l) The Careless Husband. page 20. line 26 and 34. *p.* 22, *l.* 8.

(m) Gibraltar *Sheet* E *p.* 40, line 18. with many others.

(n) Love at first Sight, *page* 43, Scene 2. with many others.

(o) Gibraltar, *page* 24, *line* 4 and 11. Sheet E p. 40, *l.* 1. Sheet G p. 56, *l.* 4. *p.* 57, *l.* 16. Hampstead Heath, *page* 53, *line* 14. Perolla and Izadora, *Epilogue line* 15, &c. Solon, page 25, *line* 28. The Amorous Miser, *page* 3, *line* 25, &c. p. 5, *l.* 23. The Basset Table, *page* 47, *line* 5. p. 55, *l.* 14. p. *ult. l.* 25. The Biter, *page* 12, *line* 2. p. 59. *l.* 25. The British Enchanters, *page* 81, *line* 28. The Confederacy, *page* 38, *line* 28. The Fair Example, *page* 59. *line* 10. The Female Wits, *page* 62, *line* 17. The Lawyer's Fortune, *page* 41, *line* 19. The Loyal Subject, *page* 47, *line* 12. The Metamorphosis, *page* 22, *line* 18. The Northen Lass, *Prologue line* 19, *Epilogue line* 23. *page* 3, *line* 19. p. 7. *l.* 8. p. 30, *l.* 29. *p.* 39. *l.* 35. p. 40, *l.* 12. p. 47, *l.* 11. p. 54, *l.* 31. p. 56. *l.* 2. p. 65, *l.* 17. The Portsmouth Heiress, *page* 10, *line* 1, &c. p. 82, *l.* 28. The Rival Brothers, *page* 78. *line* 5. p. 79, *l.* 26. Ulysses, *page* 46, *line* 3.

(p) Arsinoe, *page* 26. *line* 11. p. 45. *in fine.* The Biter, *page* 17 and page 45. The Northern Lass, *page* 44. *line penult.* p. 55. *l.* 14. The Loyal Subject, *page* 46, Song 2, and Song 4. The Quacks, *page* 28. The Royal Merchant, *page* 28, *line* 23. p. 30. *l.* 29.

Monthly Collections furnish the *Singing Masters* with *Songs*, to teach the *Ladies* for their better *Breeding*, and sometimes for their *utter Ruin*. When they use (q) *Expressions* with a *double Entendre*, they (r) have such Actions as shew their Meaning. Nay, s) such things as are forbid to be spoken, are afterward printed at large. All these *Mysteries of Iniquity* put such Notions into the Minds of the *Hearers*, and leave such Impressions, which otherwise they had not known; and which some, who ignorantly have gone to the *Play-House*, have afterwards Ingeniously confess'd. Here are all Sorts of *Love-Stories* related, to please the Fancy; and all Sorts of Devices shewn, which *Satan* can invent, to insnare and ruin the well meaning, but two unwary Girl: And when Whoremongers have learn'd their Parts on the *Stage*, they will quickly act them in another Place. In a late *Comedy*, *Fetcher* a Pimp tells his Master, [t] that he *found his Wenches for him*, and afterwards acquaints the *Audience*, how he came by this cursed Skill, [u] *I am read, I am Book-learned*. The Reason that *Pimps so often miscarry is, because* they don't

(q) The *Northern Lass*, page 66, line 2. The *Quacks*, page 26, line 25. p. 29, l, 2. The *StageCoach*, page 2, line penult.

(r) The *CarelessHusband*, page 8, line 21.

(s) The *Quacks*, *Epilogue the first*.

(t) *Gibraltar*, page 5, line 8.

(u) *Gibraltar*, Sheet E page 40, line 16.

K 3

don't read *History*, they don't grow. acquainted with *Stratagems*. I for my *Part* read *History*, and thou shalt see I'll do thy *Business* rarely. Now as (x) *Plays* by the *Poets* are accounted the Genuine History of the Age; so I suppose they are spoken of by this intreaguing *Pimp*, but I am sure they are exactly adapted for such a cursed Purpose.

(x) An Act at Oxford, *Preface* *page* 5, *line* *ult.*

The *Roving Husband reclaim'd* is a *Comedy* said to be *written by a Club* *of Ladies in Vindication of Virtuous Plays,* and printed in this present Year. I shall therefore transcribe at Length what these *modest Ladies* speak of *A-dultery*, with a *Virtuous Design*, as they tell us, to reclaim a *Roving Husband*, that the Reader may the better judge of other *Performances* upon the *Stage*.

Page 17, line 25, spoken by Women, the first married, the other single.

Tis mightily out of the Mode to love ones Husband, and 'tis Alamode to love some Body else. [Answer.] *It's a strange Fashion methinks.* [Reply.] *Only the prettiest in the World ; nothing pleases me like it.* Note that a Text of Scripture

ture is immediately quoted for Proof of this Doctrine.

Page 29, line 8. spoken by a Colonel endeavouring to debauch a married Woman.

I desire nothing from you, but what is for your good ; —— 'Tis Love! Almighty Love! has never given me Rest since I saw you. Here an Attribute of God, is ascribed to a Pagan Idol.

Page 31, line 17, spoken by a married Woman concerning Adultery.

If married Folks must have no Pleasure but from one another, they had as good be condemn'd to the Gallies, and the Town would be but a despicable Place.

Page 33, line 16, spoken by a Widow and the Colonel.

Widow.] *She* [whom the Colonel would debauch] *fancies 'tis ordained for Wives to suffer without Thought of Return.* [Colonel.] *She's much to be pitied, for she, I believe knows not what it is to be really happy,* that is, to commit Adultery. Answer Widow.] *There-*

fore

fore fhe's not to be pitied, for fhe knows not what fhe wants, or elfe I warrant fhe would not be fo backward. The Widow proceeds with a Tincture of *Smut*, which I muft omit.

Page 47, line 6, fpoken by a Man.

My Heart I can give but to one, and that muft be a Woman that neither feeks mine, nor any one's elfe ; my Body I can difpofe of in feveral Places.

Page 51, line antepenult, fpoken to a married Woman by a Lady.

Neither can I imagine what makes you take fuch Pains to be true to a Man, who is falfe to you, for to my Know-ledge, your Hufband has a Miftrefs now ready to lye in. Here a Perfon of Quali-ty is reprefented as a *Pimp.*

Page 52, line 11, fpoken by the fame Lady.

I am for the modern Way. Love a little, not long, but often ; and never make thy felf uneafy for any Man. The Virtue you boaft of fo much, I own, is a very fine thing if one could have it in-fur'd ; but it often happens Women grow weary

weary of it, when no Body cares to take it from them : And lest this should be your chance, you had as good give it [commit Adultery] while you may be thank'd for it, as keep it and cry it about the Streets when no Body will buy it.

Page 59, line 5, spoken by the Devil, rais'd by a Fortune-teller.

Just such a one is allotted for thee,
Which if you refuse you ne'er happy will
*   be :*
Ne'er think 'tis a Sin, [Adultery] of a
*   Truth I do know*
'Tis the Will of the Fates, and they will
*   have it so.*

Here *Adultery* is represented as the only way to Happiness, as irresistible, and what the Fates or *God* decrees. and is consequently the Author of. 'Tis true, this is spoken by a *Devil incarnate*, and this, I suppose, the Virtuous Authors think to be a sufficient Apology.

Page 62, line 8, spoken by the Colonel.

If you love me how can you see me dying for that which you can with so much Ease and Pleasure grant ? A Woman that is more chast than I would
*   have*

have you be, what is she good for ? A sullen thing, that makes it her Business and Pride to war with the Flesh : [according to our Baptiſmal Vow] *She has cold Blood in her Veins, perhaps, and if it be natural, 'tis a lazy Diſeaſe, and not a Virtue.*

Beſide, in this Virtuous *Play* here is contained great Store of Smut, [*y*] both in Verſe and Proſe, ſpoken without Diſtinction [*z*] by a Widow [*a*] by a Colonel, and [*b*] by a Lady of Quality. I hope the Authors intended not to affront their Modeſty, but 'tis Pity that the Ladies when they write, muſt follow the Faſhion.

[*y*] Page 40, *line* 5.
[*z*] Page 3, *line* 19.
[*a*] Page 35, *line* 6.
[*b*] Page 53, *line* 11.

If then a *Comedy* written by Ladies is offenſive, tho' they are naturally more modeſt than the other Sex, what muſt we think of ſuch as are written by Men ? If a *Comedy* written in Vindication of Virtuous *Plays* is ſcandalous, what muſt we think of thoſe who have no ſuch Deſign in View ? If it is thus with a *Play* printed after thoſe which are moſt profane have been expoſed, what muſt we think of the *Plays* when the *Poets* went on without Controul ? And if it is thus ſince the *Stage* is under Correction, and

and pretends to an extraordinary *Reformation*, what was it before Mr. *Vanbrugh* and Mr. *Congreve* took this Employment upon them?

Can any one therefore think that the Poets or *Actors* ever read or mind such Places of *Scripture* which speak against (c) *Adultery*, (d) *Fornication* and (e) *Whoredom*, and exhorts us to avoid (f) all such Discourse as hath a Tendency thereto? The *Scriptures* tell us that these *Sins* expose us to the Judgments of *God*, and tend to the Ruin both of Soul and Body; and if such Men thought hereon, they would not thus venture to debauch our Youth, and turn our Cities into so many Places like *Sodom* and *Gomorrah*, lest when others may be destroyed with Fire and Brimstone, they also should perish in the Flames. But he who compares their Practice with the *Scriptures* hath Cause to think that these Vices are so frequently promoted, because they are

(c) *Exod.* 20. 14. *Lev.* 20. 1c. *Deut.* 5. 18. *Psal.* 50. 18, 21. *Jer.* 7. 9. 0, and 13. 27, and 23. 10, 11. *Prov.* 6. 26. 32. *Ezek.* 23. 45. *Hos.* 2. 2, 3, and 4. 13, 14. *Mal.* 3 5. *Matth.* 5. 27, 28, 29, 30, and 15. 18, 19. *Mark* 7. 20, 21. *Luke* 18. 19, 20. 1 *Cor.* 6. 9, 10. *Gal.* 5. 19 21. *Heb.* 13. 4. *Jam.* 4. 3, 4. 2 *Pet.* 2. 13, 14.

(d) *Ezek.* 16. 15, 28, 29, 58, 59. *Act.* 15. 20, 29. *Rom.* 1. 21, 24, 29. 1 *Cor.* 5. 9, 10, 11. 1 *Cor.* 6. 13, 18. 2 *Cor.* 12. 21. *Colos.* 3. 5, 6. 1 *Thes.* 4. 3. *Heb.* 12. 15, 16. *Jude, verse* 7. *Rev.* 2. 20, 21, 22.

(e) *Lev.* 19. 29. *Numb.* 25. 1, 3. *Deut.* 22. 20, 21. *Deut.* 23. 17. *Prov.* 23. 27, 28. *Jer.* 13. 27. *Hos.* 4. 10, 11. *Nah.* 3. 3, 4. 1 *Tim.* 1. 9, 10. *Rev.* 21. 8, and 22. 15.

(f) 1 *Cor.* 15. 33. *Eph.* 5. 3, 4, 11, 12, and 4. 29, 30. 1 *Thes.* 5. 22.

so frequently forbidden ; and the *Actors* are so plainly guilty of corrupt Communication, because *God* hath so plainly caution'd us to avoid it.

From Fornication and all other deadly Sin, and from those who thus endeavour to promote it, Good Lord deliver us.

In our *Litany* we pray to *God* to deliver us, *from Battle and Murder, and from sudden Death.* In (*g*) the *Scriptures, Murder* and *Revenge*, and even every thing which hath a Tendency to such Crimes, are positively forbidden. Upon the *Stage*, especially in *Tragedies*, the *Hearers* are taught to delight in Blood. There is scarce a *Comedy* without Instances of Whoring, and scarce a *Tragedy* without Instances of *Murder* and *Revenge*, nay Plots and Contrivances to bring about such Designs. If the *Reader* views but one (*h*) *Act* mentioned in the Margin, he may have a small Tast of all the Rest, and perhaps may think it needless to search for more. Besides we have several Instances of self-Murder on the *Stage*, and I do not remember one which is afterward exposed as a Crime. Such Sights, *Bloodshed* and *Cruelty*,
being

(g) Exod. 20. 13. Deut. 5. 17. Gen 9. 6. Numb. 35. 30, 31. Rev. 21. 8, and 22. 15. 1 Tim. 1. 9. Gal. 5. 19. 21. Rom. 12. 18, 19, 20, 21. Matth. 5 21 to 26.

(h) Perolla and Izadora, Act 2, beginning in page 13.

being shewn on the *Stage*, do by Degrees occasion the *Spectators* to be fierce and outragious ; and Men, if I may so speak, do there learn to be inhuman. It is in this case very observable, that the greatest *Persecutions* that were ever raised against the *Christians* were begun and carried on in *Heathen Rome*, where they had their *Theatres*, and their *Tragedies* were most frequently acted. This made them more savage, and barbarous, insomuch that the Martyrdom of the *Saints* soon became their Diversion, and *Christians* were in Reality brought forth to be devoured by *wild-Beasts*, and thus make Pastime for those who had pleas'd themselves with such Resemblances. And since the *Reformation* it is as remarkable, that the dreadful Persecutions against the *Protestants*, and all the cursed Designs to destroy our *Religion* have either been begun, or at least, approved and promoted by that City. This is that *great Whore*, who hath diverted her self by the *Theatres*, and *Jubilees* ; and as she was addicted to such Sports and Pastimes, it may be the less wondred at, that in all Ages she hath made her self so *drunk with the Blood of the Saints*.

In

(*i*) *Exod.*
20. 16. *Deut.*
5. 20. *Psal.* 15.
1,3, *and* 50.16.
20, 21. *Matth.*
7. 1, 2, 3, 4,
5, 12.
In the (*i*) *Scriptures*, we are commanded to be tender of our Neighbours Reputation as well as our own, and in this as well as other Particulars to do to others as we would have them do to us. Our *Plays* abuse all Orders and Degrees of Men among us, without any manner of Distinction, and advise their *Hearers* to follow their Example.

(*k*) The
Fair Example,
page 10, *line*
31.
I shall here insert (*k*) at large, one of their Precepts to this Purpose.

When Men's Backs are turn'd, if you have any Scandal to load them with, then be sure to remember them, nay forget your own Name sooner than theirs; for let me tell you, Scandal is the very Pam in Conversation, and you should always lead it about for the good of the Board; spare no Body, every one is pleas'd to see their Neighbour loo'd: If you have but Stock enough to pay your Club in that, you may keep Company with the highest Flyer of 'em all. Nay,

(*) The Bi-
ter, *Epilogue*
page 1, *line* 28.
since they are apprehensive that (*) the *Liberty* of the *Stage* in this Respect begins to decline, and that they must not use their abusive Talents in

(†) The
Biter, *Epilogue*
page 2, *line*
penult.
publick, as formerly they have done; therefore (†) they advise others to *rail* at, and expose their Neighbours in private,

private, from the highest to the lowest, and tell us, that this is the true Way to work a *Reformation.* Their Way to reclaim one *Vice,* is by committing of another, and *Doing evil that good may come,* is esteemed among them as a *Virtue.*

In *Scripture, Pride* is represented, as a *(l)* grievous Crime, which *God resists,* which *goeth before Destruction,* which causeth *Contention* and *Shame,* and is *hateful both to God and man.* In *(m)* the *Play-House* it is represented as the only Guard to *Virtue.*

In *Scripture,* we are caution'd to avoid *(n) Rioting* and *Drunkenness,* being *Vices* unbecoming of the *Gospel,* and exclusive of *Heaven.* Upon the *Stage, (o) Drunkenness* is commended at large, and *(p)* a *Song* is sung in Praise of it. When *(q)* the *Rich Man* in the *Gospel* said to his Soul, *take thine ease, eat, drink and be merry;* then *God* call'd him *Fool,* and told him, That that very night his soul should be required of him. Upon the *Stage (r)* a mock *Justice of Peace,* instead of giving good Examples, punishing evil Doers, and rewarding such as do well, turns to these Excesses, bids *God* Defiance, argues with himself

(l) 1 *Pet.* 5. 5. *Prov.* 16. 18, *and* 13. 10, *and* 11. 2, *and* 8. 13. *Psal.* 101. 5.

(m) The Tender Husband, *page* 1, *line* 8.

(n) Deut. 29. 19, &c. *Prov.* 23. 20, 21, *and* 28. 7. *Luke* 21. 34. *Rom.* 13. 12, 13, 14. 1 *Cor.* 5. 9, 11, *and* 6. 10 *Gal.* 5. 19, 21.

(o) Love at first Sight, *pa.* 3, *line* 4, *to the End.*

(p) The Amorous, Miser, *page* 39.

(q) Luke 12. 16 *to* 22.

(r) The Northern Lass, *pa.* 38, *line* 20. *and* p. 39, *l.* 24.

himself in a *Language* directly agreeing with this *Fool*, and ushers it in, with the *Blasphemous Pretence* of his *Eyes* being opened, and an extraordinary *Revelation*.

It is therefore very evident, that the *Scriptures* and the *Stage* are directly contrary to each other. The *Scriptures* recommend *Virtue*, and the *Stage* recommends *Vice*; and as we *cannot serve God and Mammon*, because they are contrary *Masters*; so for the same *Reason*, I cannot but admire how a *Man* who believes the *Scriptures*, and pretends to *Christianity*, can take any *Pleasure* in a *Play-House* Diversion.

CHAP.

C H A P. VIII.

Superiors and others abused by the Stage.

HAving shewn in the former Chapters, how void our present *Stage* is of the Fear of *God*, I shall now speak of that Regard, which they pay to *Man*; and this upon a due Examination will be found to be of the same Piece. In short, they endeavour to censure, ridicule and expose all Men from the highest to the lowest without Distinction. All that come in their Way must be the Subject of their Scorn and Contempt, especially such as are in *Authority*.

The *Scriptures* do exhort us [a] to obey our *Superiors* in general, to pay them all possible Respect and Honour, to *render to them their due*, and tell us, that *Kings* and *Rulers* are *God's Vicegerents*, and act by his special Commission; but the *Language* of the *Stage* is of a very different Nature.

To begin therefore with *crown'd Heads*. The *Stage* pretends to have *Patents* from such to act; and therefore,

(a) *Exod.* 20. 12. *Deut.* 5. 16. *Matth.* 22. 21. *Rom.* 13. 1, 2, 3, 4, 5, 6, 7. 1 *Tim.* 5. 17, 18. *Heb.* 13. 7, 17. 1 *Pet.* 2. 13, 14.

L

fore, tho' *Religion* muſt be kick'd out of Door, yet one would think, that either *Gratitude* or *Intereſt* might teach them better Manners. 'Tis true, they ſet themſelves up for the Schools of good *Breeding* and fine *Language*: But as our *Saviour* tells us, we *do not gather grapes of thorns, nor figs of thiſtles*; and we muſt not expect, that they who act ſo rudely themſelves, can teach others Civility. The *Beam* is *in their eyes*, and therefore till this is caſt out, they are very unfit to diſcover ſuch a *Moth in another Man's*; and indeed, it is neceſſary that they ſhould reform themſelves, before they pretend to give Example for others to imitate.

The *firſt* Inſtance which I ſhall mention, is the more remarkable, becauſe we are told in the *Title-Page*, that it was ſpoken at the *Queens Theatre*, by one of *Her Majeſties* ſworn Servants. The Words are [*b*] theſe.

Imperial Drones, that with luxurious Eaſe
Securely loll upon their lazy Thrones,
And never think from whence their ſafety
    comes:
Tho' thouſands nobly Sacrifice their Lives
To guard their Crowns, or but increaſe
    Power,
                    Yet

Yet see the Recompence of all their Toils;
The Gratitude of Kings.

What Service this is to *Her Majesty,*
I do not apprehend.   The *Actors* tax
a *crown'd Head* with *Negligence* and
Ingratitude, and then leave a disaffect-
ed *Auditor* to make the Application,
and suggest to others in private the
Words which are thus spoken in publick.   In one (c) *Tragedy Rhoderique* the
King is represented as a most inhuman
Ravisher of an innocent *Virgin.*   In (d)
others, the Kings are represented as
hearkning to all manner of evil Council, and punishing their best Friends,
until thereby they procure the Hatred
of their Subjects, and bring themselves
to the Brink of Ruin.   In some
Tragedies the Kings and Emperors are
deposed.   In some they are mur-
dered.   In others, *Plots* are carried on
against them, and frequently with
Success, lest *Traitors* should despair in
forming their Enterprizes; besides we
are told, that (f) *in Rebellion, Success*
avows the Fact, and a *Rebel* (g) in the
midst of these Conspiracies cries out,
Oh for a Crown! I will about the glo-
rious Enterprize : and all this, as Mr.

(c) The Conquest of Spain, *page* 15, *line* 24. *p.* 23, *l.* 9, &c.

(d) The Faithful General, *page* 8, *line* 10. *p.* 9, *l.* 9. The Loyal Subject, *page* 30, *line* 20.

(e) *Page* 56, *line ult.*

(f) The Portsmouth, Heiress, *page* 13. *line* 18.

(g) Solon, *page* 23, *line* 14, *Scene* Athens, *a Common Wealth.*

L 2   *Dennis*

(*h*) His
Usefulness of
the Stage, from
page 49, to pa.
69.

Dennis obferves (*h*) is very ferviceable to the *Englifh Government*. However, it is well that our *Laws*, and the Senfe of our Duty work ftronger on the Fancy than thefe Reprefentations, otherwife we know not what might be the Confequence. In (*i*) one

(*i*) The
Faithful, General, page 18,
line 26.

Tragedy, *Galerius* the *Emperor* kneels to his Miftrefs, and is affronted by her, without fhewing any Refentment, nay,

(*k*) Page
34 line 13.

he (*k*) afterward fneaks down into the fame Pofture with Words more fubmiffive than before. In another, *Hannibal* is reprefented both as a *King* and

[*l*] Perolla
and Izadora,
page 63, line
34.

a *General*, and yet [*l*] he is publickly and fcandaloufly affronted.

These are Foreign Examples, yet they may have a Domeftick Influence: However, Inftances neater Home may be produced. *Her Majefty* was gracioufly pleas'd to fend Her Forces to *Cadis* under the Command of the *Duke of Ormond*, to attack the Enemy on that fide, with Hopes of Succefs. It happened that fome of the *Soldiers* abufed the *Nuns* and other Women, in fuch a Manner, as alienated the Affections of the *Spaniards*, and fo the Defign mifcarried. The next Year *Sir George Rook* attacqued and took
Gibraltar

Gibraltar. The *Cadis* Expedition and the Cause of the Miscarriage was a Subject very unfit for *Comedy* in the *English* Nation ; in *Spain* it might have pleas'd *The Duke of Anjou.* However, here we have a *Play* call'd *Gibraltar,* representing all the *English Souldiers,* as addicted to Whoredom, and one would think, it was designed to bid the *Spaniards* beware. In this *Comedy,* to shew that the *Officers* are all alike, there are only two *English Colonels, viz. Wilmot* and *Vincent,* who endeavour to debauch *Leonora* and *Jacquelinda,* two *Spanish Ladies,* declaring against Marriage. Nay, they tell them [m] that the *Women are afraid of their Liberty, as well as the Men* ; as if the Liberty aim'd at, was only to make them Whores. This was written by Mr. *Dennis,* who knew the *Usefulness of Plays to the* English *Government.* However, blessed be *God,* we have better Success, and our *Soldiers* behaved themselves in another Manner ; but no thanks is due to the *Poet* or *Stage,* who made a Jest of that, for which all others sorry in earnest.

(m) *Sheet* E *page* 33, *line penult.*

The *French* being beaten at *Hockstead* and *Ramellies,* the Siege of *Bar-*

L 3 *celona*

(*a*) *This was published since the 10th Day of March last, and therefore I have not mentioned many other exceptionable Passages, which are in it.*

(*b*) *The Conclusion being in Verse, and the Summ of all, page 72, line 34.*

(*c*) *The Title Page.*

(*d*) *Wednesday July the 24th, and Thursday July the 25th, 1706.*

(*e*) *Page 28, line 26. p. 32, l. 4.*

(*f*) *Page 32, line 25.*

(*g*) *Page 29, line 10. p. 31, l. 31.*

(*h*) *Page 3, line 29. p. 5, l. 21. p. 6, l. 22 and 35. p. 7, l. 1 and 9. p. 13, l. 30. p. 23. l. penult*

(*i*) *Page 4, line 1.*

(*k*) *Page 3, line 29.*   (*l*) *Page 4, line 11.*
(*m*) *Page 4, line 15.*

celona being raifed in *Spain*, and our *Generals* gaining the Love of that Nation, by a more prudent Behaviour in a fecond Expedition, there was no Way to oblige the common Enemy, and prevent our farther Succeffes, except by hindering *the Raifing of Recruits* for the *Army*. Accordingly, there was lately publifhed a *Comedy* call'd (*a*) *The Recruiting Officer*, (*b*) to render this Employment as odious as poffible. This was acted in *London* (*c*) by fome who ftile themfelves *Her Majefties Servants*, and alfo in (*d*) *Briftol*, whilft others were beating up for *Volunteers*. Here one *Captain* is reprefented as a (*e*) notorious Lyar, another as (*f*) a Drunkard, one (*g*) intreagues with Women, another (*h*) is fcandaloufly guilty of *debauching* them; and tho the *Serjeant* was (*i*) married to five Women before, yet the *Captain* perfwades him to (*k*) marry another, as a Cloak for fuch Roguery, (*l*) to make up his five Wives half a Dozen, and (*m*) to cheat the *Queen*, by entering a Child born the Day before into the Mufter-Roll, and after all he ftiles thefe

De-

Debaucheries (*n*) *an Air of Freedom, which People mistake for Lewdness, as they mistake Formality in others for Religion,* and then proceeds in commending his own Practice, and exposing the other. In this *Play* the *Officers* are represented as (*o*) quarrelsom, but (*p*) Cowards. The *Serjeant* (*q*) makes the *Mob* drunk to list them, (*r*) gives two of them two Broad Pieces of Gold, for Pictures, and finding the Mony upon them, pretends that they are listed: At another Time he is (*s*) ready to swear any thing for the Good of the Service; and also (*t*) perswades Men to list in the Disguise of a *Conjurer,* with (*u*) most profane Language in Commendation of the *Devil;* and all this is to make good the saying of *Virgil* inserted in the Title Page, *Captiq; dolis, donisq;coacti.* In this *Play* (*x*) the *Officers* confess, that they greatly abuse the new listed *Soldiers ;* (*y*) *Debauching* of the Country Wenches is represented as a main Part of the Service; All the private Centinels are guilty of (*z*) stealing Horses, Sheep and Fowls, and (*a*) the *Captain* desires, that he may have but one honest Man in the Company for the Novelty's sake. After this the

(*n*) Page 41, line 27.

(*o*) Page 36, line 31.
(*p*) Page 37, line 6.
p. 58, l. 37.
(*q*) Page 18, line 6.
(*r*) Page 19, line 4.
(*s*) Page 65, line 33.
(*t*) Page 45, line 1.

(*u*) Page 50, line 15, and 32.

(*x*) Page 26, line 1.
p. 66, l. 16.
(*y*) Page 40, line 29.
(*z*) Page 58, line 24.
(*a*) Page 63, line 13.

L 4 *Justices*

Justices of the Peace are made the Jest of the *Stage*, for (*b*) discharging their Duty in listing of Soldiers, and the *Constable* (*c*) hath a Lash into the Bargain, that no one who serves his Country on this Occasion, may escape the *Play-House* Censure. Some of their Expressions relating to the *Officers* of the Army will shew us the Temper, Fine Language, and Gratitude of the *Stage*.

(*b*) Page 61, line 1, to the End of the Play.

(*c*) Page 65, line 24, &c.

Page 55, line 9. Of *Generals.*

You never knew a great General in your Life, that did not love a Whore.

Page 35, line 2. Of *Field-Officers.*

You shall receive your Pay, and do no Duty. [Answer]*Then you must make me a Field-Officer.*

Page 31, line 3, Of all other *Officers.*

The Officers every Year bring over a Cargo of Lace, to cheat the Queen of her Duty, and the Subjects of their Honesty.

Page 31, line 16.

The

The Officers are curs'd, saying, that *they do the Nation more Harm, by Debauching us at Home, than they do good by Defending us abroad.*

Page 38, line 3. Of *Captains.*

A bold Step — (d) --- *and an impudent Air are the principal Ingredients in the Composition of a Captain.*

(d) Here are two smutty Entenders in the Characters of a Captain, which must be omitted.

Page 25, line 36. Of *Serjeants,* spoken by a *Serjeant.*

Cast up the whole Sum, viz. *Canting, Lying, Impudence, Pimping, Bullying, Swearing, Whoring, Drinking, and an Halbard, and you will find the Sum Total will amount to a Recruiting Serjeant.*

Page 6, line 31, spoken of *Recruiting Officers,* by a *Captain* employed in this Business.

What! No Bastards! and so many Recruiting Officers in Town! I thought 'twas a Maxim among them to leave as many Recruits in the Country as they carried out.

It may be observed, That when the *Souldiers* were guilty of *Immoralities* in *Spain*, they were caress'd by the *Stage*, and there crown'd with Success; but now we hear of no such Complaints, they are censur'd and ridicul'd. When they really were debauch'd, they were never thus affronted; but since the Endeavours used to reform the Army, they are thus expos'd. The greater and more signal the Services are, which they do the Nation, the more the *Play-Houses* shew their Resentments; and whilst others justly applaud them for their Merits, the *Poets* and *Actors* are the only Persons who thus lampoon them. What Thanks are due to such Men from the *French King* I shall not determine, but I am sure, that they deserve none from the *English Government*; and if neither Mr. *Dennis* nor this *Author* can render the *Stage* more useful, we are not, in the least, beholden for their Assistance. I suppose, that both the *Queen*, *Lords* and *Commons* have different Sentiments concerning the Merits of the *Officers*; and These who stile themselves in Print, *Her Majesty's Servants*, are the only Men, who publickly undervalue such as hazard their Lives *in Her Majesty's Service*. Nei-

Neither do they censure the *Officers* and *Army* alone; but all who belong to the *Court* are vilify'd, expos'd and ridicul'd. We are told at the *Play-House*, [n] That there is *no Truth at Court*; That [o] *a Man in publick Trust, now and then performs one Action with the nicest Punctilio of Honour imaginable, that he may the more unsuspected play forty Knavish ones.* That [p] *the Courtiers run out of Town to avoid their Creditors,* and [q] *Want and Age hath made some of them great Husbands and Civil; but sometimes a new Debauch, and a fluttering Fellow creeps in, to make some Laughter.* They tell us, that [r] *the Generals now are wiser than in former Ages, and know how to spin out the War to the best Advantage.* That [s] *it is so unlike a Gentlewoman to talk with a Religious Air, that a Country Lady, who had been three short Minutes at Court, would be asham'd to talk so, when she went down again to her Husband;* nay, That [t] *Vice by the Dexterity of our Councils is made the Supporter of Religion and the Laws.* At one time they tells us, That [u] *there are Places at Court and in the Army, but none to be had without Mony;* But at another Time, That [x] *if a Man*

(n) Love for Love, re-printed, 1704 page 57, line 31.

(o) The Humour of the Age, printed 1701, page 4, line 32.

(p) Tunbridge Walks, printed 1703, page 1, line 5.

(q) The Lawyers Fortune, page 38, line 19.

(r) Solon, page 6, line 19.

(s) Love at first Sight pg. 14, line 21.

(t) Gibraltar, page 6, line 21.

(u) The Lawyers Fortune, page 29. line 15.

(x) Solon, page 46, line 29.

(y) An Act
at Oxford, pa.
10, line 15.
Hampstead
Heath, page
12, line 29.

(z) An Act
at Oxford, pa.
49, line 33.
can neither write nor read, yet if he can
say Ay or No with the Croud, he'll make
a good Senator; and That [y] *Hungry
Resolution, some Assurance and no Principles are the three great Steps to modern
Preferment;* Nay, [z] a Man must be very
dull in Publick to qualify himself for it.

The Late Revolution was the visi-
ble *Method* of God's *Providence* to res-
cue this *Church* and *Nation* from im-
minent Danger, and preserve to us our
Religion, *Laws* and *Liberties*; and yet
this signal Mercy is (a) ridicul'd and
burlesqu'd upon the *Stage* in a scandalous Manner.

Mr. *Collier* in his Reply to Mr.
Congreve, page 74, tells us, that *Stage
Princes are never represented insignificant, treated with Contempt, and play'd
the Fool with in Comedy. If they were
thus us'd* (saith he) *I question not,
but that the* Poets *and* Players *would
quickly hear on't.* But now they take
a Liberty, unknown to him or former
Ages, and treat both *Crown'd Heads,*
and their *Courts,* with the same Scurrility, which they bestow on other Persons.

The next Compliments which they
pay are to the *Nobility.* When *Plays*
are guilty of *Swearing, Cursing, Blasphemy,*
Smut,

Smut and Profaneneſs, they are [b] frequently dedicated to a *Perſon of Quality,* that such a one may patronize
them. This is rather a Affront than
a Token of Respect. It is a Representing of them by Name, as Encouragers
or Abettors of *Vice* and *Profaneneſs.*
Besides, the Expreſſions in these *Epiſtles*
are very remarkable. He who designs
to write a *Burleſque,* or *Satyr* in Prose
on any Woman, because she is affected,
Proud, and Self-conceited, hath an excellent Pattern in a [c] late Dedication. One of the *Poets* wisheth, [d]
that his *Patron* may live 'til every
Body, and even his best Friends are
weary of him, and then, I confeſs, it
is high Time to think of Death. The
Author of *The Careleſs Huſband* repre-
sents only two *Lords* in his *Play,* one
is the most ridiculous *Fop* in Nature,
and the other a most notorious *Whore-
monger,* and yet he complements a *Duke*
in his *Epiſtle* with these Words, *I owe
moſt of it, to the many ſtolen Obſerva-
tions, I have made from your Grace's
Manner of Converſing.* Certainly, these
Poets deserve the best Rooms in *Bedlam.*
I do not wonder that they lose their
Wits when they write *Plays,* because
they

(b) An Act
at Oxford,
Perolla and L-
zadora,
The Baſſet
Table,
The Lying
Lover,
The Northern
Laſs,
Ulyſſes.

(c) The
Faithful Ge-
neral.

(d) The
Gameſter.

they have not enough left to frame an *Epistle*. Since the Liquor of *Parnassus* intoxicates their Brains, a dry Diet, and a Dose of *Hellebore* will do much better, and then they may sleep till they are sober.

To pass on to the *Plays* themselves. They (*e*) first in the *Drama*, mention the *Lords* by ridiculous Names, and then make them as guilty as the rest, of *Swearing, Cursing, Whoring,* and all Sorts of *Debauchery.* Here we are told that (*f*) their *Skulls are empty*, (*g*) they *secure Mony for their Mistresses when they are weary of their Wives*, and it is *scandalous* among them *to love their Wives above half a Year*; That (*h*) their *Honour is lazy*, and their *Breeding beggerly*; That (*i*) they are so poor, that *Six may be broke for six Pistoles*; That (*k*) *Persons of great Quality have no Sense*; (*l*) *their Speeches are Counterfeit*; (*m*) their *Wives are Whores*; (*n*) it is their *Prerogative to ruin Tradesmen*, especially *with an honourable Air*; they are (*o*) *foolish Fellows*,

(e) The Careless Husband, *Person* 1 and 2. The Female Wits, *Person* 5, and 6. The Gamester, *Person* 8. The Roving Husband reclaim'd, *Person* 3.
(f) The Roving Husband, &c. *pa.* 4, *line* 8.
(g) Idem, *p* 25. *line* 15.
(h) An Act at Oxford, *page* 22, *line* ult.
(i) An Act at Oxford, *pa.* 19 *line* 25.
(k) As you find it, *printed* 1703. *page* 13, *line* 25.
(l) Ibid, *page* 24, *line* 9.
(m) Love at first Sight, *page* 6, *line* 17.
(n) The Basset Table, *page* 49, *line* 2.
(o) The Careless Husband, *page* 13, *line* 37.

and

and (*p*) *never in Love with the Women they would marry*; they (*q*) *pay no Body*, (*r*) *insult every Body*, (*s*) *abuse* and *affront them, ruin their Reputation, kick* others *out of Doors, when they come to ask for their own*, and (*t*) spend their Mony in *Gaming*, with (*u*) many other *horrid* and *scandalous* Reflections.

(*p*) Ibid. line 27.

(*q*) The Confederacy, page 3, line 25.

(*r*) The Careless. Husband, page 22, line 19

(*s*) The Confederacy page 9, line 9.

(*t*) The Confederacy, page 15, line 32. The Gamester page 28, line 14. p. 32, l. 1.

(*u*) The Careless Husband, page 17, line 32. p. 19, l. 23. The Confederacy, page 2, line 22.

The next Respect, which I shall mention, is that which they pay to such as put the *Laws* in Execution, from the Highest to the Lowest, especially against *Immorality* and *Profaneness*. The *Players* were prosecuted for their Misbehaviour, and found *Guilty*. At this they snarl and rave, and cannot forbear their Resentments. I suppose, that their *Hearers*, being so well aquainted with their *Oaths* and *Curses*, have paid in another Place for what they learn'd at the *Play-House*, and therefore the *Magistrates* must be ridicul'd. Of this I have giv'n some Account already in the *first Chapter*, and need not repeat what is there mention'd.

To

To begin with the *Judges*. These act by *Her Majesty's Commission*, and therefore the Affronts pass'd upon them have a double Stroke. Thus they insult the *Royal Authority*, as well as such who are employed thereby. When a *Judge* is represented, the very (*x*) *Name* must be ridiculous. They give him this Character, that he is (*y*) *antient* and *hard hearted*, (*z*) *sparing of his Words and Sentences*, *nodding on the Bench, with a tedious dull Plea before him*: Nay, the (*a*) going into *Westminster-Hall*, or into any other throughout their *Circuits*, is represented so very ridiculous, that I am asham'd to relate it.

Mr. Collier in his *Reply to Mr. Dennis*, page 123 concerning the *Abuse of the Clergy* by the *Stage* hath these Words, *When the Badge of a Man's Office which should give him Credit is shewn ridiculous, I fancy he has Reason to complain. If the Poet is of another Mind, let him practise the same Liberty upon a Judge or a Lord Mayor, and see how the Jest will take.* He then thought that they would not dare to do it; but we now see that they dare to do any thing.

Neither do the *Aldermen* escape any better than the *Judges*. Their Election

(*x*) An Act at Oxford, *page* 16, *line* 18.

(*y*) The Confederacy *page* 2, *line* 22.

(*z*) Love at first Sight, *page* 53, *line* 16.

(*a*) An Act at Oxford, *page* 16, *line* 18.

lection is thus defcrib'd (*b*) *Being cramb'd up into Offices among the Worfhipful,* and that of a Mayor, *at leaft upon the City's Charge made drunk for a whole Year.* Thefe have alfo (*c*) ridiculous Names, and fometimes (*d*) as ridiculous *Epithets.* They are rank'd with (*e*) *Taylors,* nay with *Pimps and* (*f*)*Pickpockets,* and defcribed as fuch, who (*g*) will *give Mony* for *Titles* of *Honour,* who (*h*) take *Bribes,* and excufe all *Offenders* that can but pay. Such who (*i*) *wifh one another at the Devil,* are in the *Poets Language* fit for *Aldermen.* One Quotation at large may be fufficient in this Cafe, taken out of *The Carelefs Hufband, Prologue the firft, line* 7.

—*Cheats and Cuckolds, Aldermen and Cullies.*

Thefe are the Company which the *Poet* thinks fit for *Aldermen*: and when he defcribes them, he tells us, that they are all alike without Diftinction, that they are

Creatures a Mufe fhould fcorn, fuch abject Trafh
Deferves not Satyr's, but the Hangman's Lafh. M *Wretches*

(*b*) The Faithful Gene-ral, *page* 41, *line* 45.
(*c*) The Tender Huf-band, *page* 21, *line* 25.
(*d*) An Act at Oxford, *pa.* 30, *line* 1. Love the Le-veller, *page* 6, *line* 15. The Lawyers For-tune, *page* 11, *line* 28.
(*e*) The Lawye.s For-tune, *page* 12, *line* 3.
(*f*) An Act at Oxford, *pa.* 17, *line* 4. Hampftead, Heath, *page* 19, *line* 12.
(*g*) Love the Leveller, *page* 6, *line* 15.
(*h*) Squire Trelooby, *Prologue, pa.* 2, *line* 3.
(*i*) The Fair Example, *page* 2, *line* 10.

*Wretches so far shut out from Sense of
    Shame,
Newgate or Bedlam only can reclaim.*

(*k*) An
Act at Ox-
ford, *Drama
Name* 4.
Hampstead
Heath, *Dra-
ma, Name* 4.
The Nor-
thern Lass,
*Drama,
Name* 3 *and*
4.

The next are the *Justices of the
Peace* in the Country. These are also
mentioned by [*k*] ridiculous Names,
represented as [*l*] exposing themselves,
and affronted by others in some whole
Pages together, with all imaginable
Rudeness, and call'd [*m*] *The Reforming
Justices, who make* at least 200 *l. per
Annum, of Whores and Pickpockets.*

(*l*) The Humour of the *Age, printed* 1701, *page* 5, &c.
page 14, &c. *and page* 38, &c. An Act at Oxford, *page* 37.
Hampstead Heath, *page* 41.

[*m*] An Act at Oxford, *page* 56, *line* 19. Hampstead
Heath, *page* 57, *line* 28.

(*) Page
27, *line* 3.

In *The Metamorphosis* [*] *Roger*
puffed up with Conceit of his being
transform'd into a Gentleman, cannot
forbear making his Reflections on this
Occasion. *When* [saith he] *I am in the
Commission of the Peace and Quorum,
I will get me a Clark, a good sensible
Fellow, much wiser than my Worship,
he shall do all the Business, and I'll have
all the Credit, and the best half of the
Fees.*

In

In *The Northern Lass*, Sir *Paul* is introduced as a *Justice of the Peace*, who was at first very zealous to reform the *Vices* of the Age, but soon turns to be a great *Debauchee* after serious Debates and Resolutions. He then tells the Audience, that [n] *he will take a new Course of Life* directly, and *blasphemously* pretends to *Illuminations*, as if the *Scripture* Notion of Repentance was a Turning from Virtue to Vice; for he accordingly resolves upon *Rioting, Drunkenness* and *Whoring*. His arguing with himself is remarkable, to [o] turn Prodigal in Point of Conscience and Equity, and [p] caress the Debauchees as Men of the greatest Virtue. After this *Vexbem* the Constable brings [q] a *Whore* before Sir *Paul*; he imprisons the Constable, [r] and saith, *Now, Lady, whereas you were brought before me as a Delinquent, I retain you as my Mistress.* Accordingly [s] he provides for her, is [t] very angry because she is stol'n away for a Fortune, then [u] he is jested at for being a Commissioner of the Peace, [x] taken in Search for this Whore in a *Spaniards* Habit, [y] carried to his own House for *Justice*, where he is ridiculously treated,

[n] *Page* 37, *line* 16.

[o] *Page* 38, *line* 20.
[p] *Page* 39, *line* 24.
[q] *Page* 46.
[r] *Ibid line* 31.
[s] *Page* 56, *in fine*
[t] *Page* 63.
[u] *Ibid line* 23.
[x] *Page* 69.

[y] *Ibid line* 33.

M 2   treated,

(*z*) *Page* 71, *line* 12.
(*a*) *Ibid* line 40.

treated, then [*z*] he abuseth another *Magistrate* by the Name of *Upstartical Justice* and [*a*] at last bribes the Constable to silence his Information.

This Example is so full that I need not add any more, neither can we

[*b*] An Act at Oxford, page 5, line 1. Hampstead Heath, *page* 5, *line* 9.

wonder after this, that they abuse all other Inferior Officers. The Principal among those who stick in their Stomacks are the *Informers*. The *Ma-*

,, [*c*] An Act at Oxford, *pa.* 29. *line* 33.

gistrates act only by Evidence, and therefore, if these can be but discou-

[*d*] An Act at Oxford, *p.* 56. *line* 19.

raged, the Laws and all other *Officers* will signify nothing. Accordingly,

[*e*] An Act at Oxford, *pa.* 23, *line* 9. *p.* 24, *l.* 11, 17, 25.

both in *The Act at Oxford*, and in *Hampstead Heath, Driver* is represented as a *Reformer of Manners*, and informs the Audience, that he is [*b*] a

[*f*] *Ibid.*

Scourge to publick Lewdness, but pri-

[*g*] An Act at Oxford, *pa* 3, *line penult.* Hampstead Heath, *page* 3, *line* 24.

vately in Love with Whoring, and a *Member of the Calves-Head-Club*, that he is [*c*] *Cursedly Malicious*, and [*d*] *makes Two Hundred Pounds a Year of*

[*h*] An Act at Oxford, *pa* 37, *line* 28. Hampstead, Heath. *page* 42, *line* 20.

Whores and Pick-Pockets. After this, he is represented as guilty of [*e*] *Cursing*, and [*f*] is buffeted and abused. Others speak of him, as a [*g*]

[*i*] An Act at Oxford. *page* 50, *line* 1.

City-Reformer, and chief Begger-Hunter, as [*h*] *Carrion fit only for Crows to feed upon*, that [*i*] such a Man is *impudent*

pudent, even to a Proverb, a [*k*] *Canting* Fellow; with *no more Religion than an English Whore*, one who is [*l*] *in Want*, and accordingly *swears* for no other Reason but a Maintainance.

(*k*) The Lawyers Fortune, *page* 9, *line* 12.

(*l* The Faithful Bride of Granada, E. pilogue, *line* 10.

The Design of forming *Societies for Reformation of Manners* (*m*) met with the Approbation of most of the *Lords*, both *Spiritual* and *Temporal*, and also the *Judges* in *England* and *Ireland*; the *Design* thereof they own'd to be *so truly Great and Noble, so much for the Honour of God, and the Advancement of Piety and Vertue, and the publick Good, both of Church and State, that* they supposed *it could not fail of being approv'd by all good Men.* And yet these very *Societies* are subject to the *Play-House* Scorns. (*n*) *What signifies,* faith an Actor, *your Reforming Society? The noble Exploit of demolishing a poor Sunday Apple-Stall!* Here is *Impiety* against *God*, as well as *Disrespect* to *Man.* A Care for the Observance of the *fourth Commandment*, according to them signifies nothing; and indeed they aim to destroy, not only that, but all the rest.

(*m*) An Account of the Societies for Reformation of Manners, *immediately after the Title page.*

(*n*) Hampstead Heath, *pa.* 5, *line* 11.

As to their Treatment of *Juries*, *Bayliffs*, and other *Officers*, I shall give but one Quotation of each, becauſe I have treſpaſſed ſo long already upon this Subject.

The Juries,

(ο) An Act at Ox-ford, *page* 29, *line* 31. Hampſtead Heath, *page* 33, *line* 19.

(ο) *I*, ſaith an Actor, *am one of the Grand Jury, and conſequently damn'd malicious, and can hang thee right or wrong.*

The Bayliffs,

(p) An Act at Ox-ford, *page* 9, *line* ult.

(p) *A Middleſex Bomb-Bayliff is an Impudence ten Degrees beyond the Devil.*

Other Officers,

(q) An Act at Ox-ford, *page* 8, *line* 22.

(q) *Are you fit to appear in Offices in this Saint-like Age? A notorious lewd Liver, and a Scandal to Reformation!* To this it is anſwer'd, *Why? Who is fitter to be employ'd, than he that ſupports the Trade of the Nation?* Here *Vice* is careſs'd, as our Support, and neceſſary for Trade, and could the *Act-ors* have their Will, the moſt *Profligate Wretches* ſhould have all the Places of Truſt, and *Profaneneſs* ſhould be a Qualification for Preferment.

The Treatment of the *Clergy* upon the *Stage* is yet more remarkable. They are the Embaſſadors of *God* and *Chriſt*, and accordingly have the ſame Uſage. 'Tis true, that ſince *God* is blaſphem'd, *Chriſt undervalu'd, and Re-ligion*

ligion undermin'd, those who are in that sacred Function may be more easy under it. *It is enough for the disciple that be be as his master, and the servant as his lord;* and therefore since they vilify the *master of the house, how much more* will they do the same by *those of his houshold?* If the Account which the *Stage* gives of the *Clergy,* be true, they are the greatest Monsters in Nature, the Bane of Mankind, the Contrivers of all Sorts of Mischief, and there is no Wickedness, but they have the greatest Hand in it. We are told by (r) a *Stage Poet,* that *Priests of all Religions are the same:* And therefore what they speak of one is easily applied to all the rest; Nay, is usually spoken in such general Terms, as may be applied without any Alteration. One would think, that all Sorts of *Religion* are a Detriment to the *Stage,* and therefore they are willing to expose them all. The *Clergy of the Church of England* makes the most considerable Figure in the Nation, and therefore they are the most censur'd and reflected on. They are spoken of on the *Stage,* as Persons who must joyn the *Lovers* in *Marriage,* and this is

(r) Dryden *in his* Absalom and Achitophel.

M 4   well

well known to be an Office, peculiar to those of the *Church of England.* Accordingly, they are *(s)* mentioned with ridiculous Names, and *(t)* frequently compar'd to *Hangmen* and *Executioners.* The Affronts put upon them, mentioned in *(u)* the Margin, are too many to be transcrib'd, and such as need the Patience of the *Church of England* to bear with them. The *(x) Diffenting Teachers* under the Name of *Spiritual Elders* fare but little better, tho' not so often mention'd. *Testimony* in *(y) Sir Courtly Nice* is brought in guilty of *Whoring* and gross *Hypocrisy,* and makes a dishonourable *Exit.* The *Prologue* in *The Stage Beaux toss'd in a Blanket,* lasheth the *Clergy* of the *Church of England,* and the *Diffenting Teachers* in a Style scandalous to the highest Degree; insomuch that the *Author* is oblig'd to excuse himself by unusual *Annotations:* And when the *Auditors* have suck'd in the vilest Opinions imaginable of both Perswasions,

(s) An Act at Oxford, *page* 36, *line* 22. The Amorous Miser, *page* 56, *in fine.* The Lawyer's Fortune, *pa.* 67, *line* 5.

(t) Love's Contrivance printed 1703 *page* 34, *line* 23. The Portsmouth Heiress, *pa.* 72, *line* 22.

(u) An Act at Oxford, *page* 36, *line* 22. *p.* 40, *l.* 9. *p.* 45, *l.* 29. Hampstead Heath, *page* 45, *line* 9. Squire Trelooby, *Prologue, line* 17. *Epilogue, line* 15. The Amorous Miser, *page* 54, *line* 6. *p.* 56, *l. antepenult and p.* 58, *l.* 30. The Gamester, *page* 61, *line* 11. The Portsmouth Heiress, *page* 7, *line* 3 and *p.* 41, *l.* 21. The Mistake, *page* 50, *line* 10. The Stage Coach, *page* 3, *line* 6. The Royal Merchant, *page* 24, *line* 15.

(x) The Portsmouth Heiress, *page* 30, *line* 21.

(y) Reprinted 703, *page* 58, 59 and 61, *to the End.*

the

the Margin in Print is thought enough to salve the Matter, tho' never heard on the *Stage*. The *Author* of *Don Sebastian* renders the *Mufti* among the *Turks*, as ignominious as he can, and exposeth the *Spanish Fryar* in the same Manner. Thus also *Love the Leveller*, and *The Faithful General* treat the *Priests* among the *Heathen*. In short, the Quotations are almost endless. No *Teacher* of *Religion* can escape this Lash, let him be of *The Church of England* or a *Dissenter*, *Protestant* or *Papist*, *Turk* or *Pagan*. Here we are taught, that they are all alike, all *Rogues* and *Villains*; and therefore what is said of one, the *Reader* may interpret of any as he pleaseth. *Teachers* of any Perswasions are expos'd, and (z) *Atheists* are recorded as the brave *Examples* for us *to follow*. In *Love the Leveller* (a) the *Author* discovers some *horrid Impieties*, which he fathers upon the *Priests of Isis*; and would gladly excuse his Mismanagement with a *Non putàram* in the *Preface*. However, his Expressions are in general Terms, and the *High Priest* is so kind, as to discover the *Author's* Design, by talking of (b) *Cannon Bullets* and Gun-

(z) Love at first Sight, *page 9, line* 3.

(a) Page 20, *line* 14. p. 25, l. 3 and 30. p. 27, l. 22, p. 29, l. 11. p. 30, l. 21. p. 31, l. 2. p. 37, l. 28. p. 38, l. 24. p. 49, l. 3. p. 50, l. 21. p. 52, l. 3 and p. 57, l. 9.

(b) Page 38, line 24.

Gunpowder, the Use whereof is well known in *England*, but was never heard of in *Ægypt*, whilst the *Priests of Isis* were there : Nay, had the *High Priest* kept the *Poet's* Counsel, yet the Walls betray him; and one of the *Scenes*, being (c) a *Chocolate-House*, brings the *Plot* nearer Home, and shews, that at least there was a double Entendre.

(c) *Page*

    The *Author* of *The Faithful General* lays the *Scene* at *Byzantium* in *Greece*; but when the *Actors* speak of the *Priests*, they use a greater Latitude in their Expressions. I shall therefore transcribe some of them at large, that the *Reader* make his own Reflections.

Page 26, line 14.

Thy Dreaming Priesthood.

Page 43, line 22.

—— *None dare dispute*
The sacred Slander, *when the Priestly*
   Power
Hath preach'd and pray'd it into Orthodox.
Nay should the Emperor himself oppose it,
They'l represent him as the People's Foe,
Make him Conspirator against himself,
And prove it is Religion to dethrone him.
               'Tis

'Tis an old pious Fraud, but still it takes.
Such Doctrine suits a Rabble. *Answer,*
  And a Priest
Both are alike for Faction, fiery, rash,
Still prone to change, and ever in the
  wrong.
No Arts the Prince and People can divide,
'Till you engage the Priesthood on your side:

Page 49 line 40.

—— 'Twas but an Oath,
And Interest may unbind that feeble Tye,
That Case the pious Priesthood have re-
  solv'd:

Page 56 line 22.

Yet still our Teachers would our Reason
  blind,
And prove, Almighty Justice rules Man-
  kind;
But should we plead from this unequal
  Doom,
They would refer us to a World to come.
Unerring Guides they all pretend to be,
Yet know as little of the Way as we.

  This is a two edged Sword, and
strikes not only at the *Clergy,* but also
at the *Providence, Power,* and *Justice*
  of

of that *God*, whose Servants they are; and was not he a *God* infinite in *Mercy*, he would make them *Examples* to others, and *Objects* of his *Justice*.

Were the *Clergy* Profane and Debauched in their Lives and Conversations, I doubt not but they would be caress'd by the *Poets*, and commended in the *Plays*. We are told (*a*) in *short*, that *no Man can be so truly Virtuous, as he who hath been truly acquainted with Vice*, and by the same Consequence the most profligate Wretches would be the fittest for Holy Orders. If the *Bishops* would take this Method in their *Ordinations*, and expect *Testimonies* of lewd, rather than of sober Behaviour, the *Clergy* then may please the *Stage*; but because (blessed be *God*) it is not so, therefore they are the Objects of their utmost Scorn and Contempt.

(*d*) Love at firstSight, page 16, line 36.

I confess (to do the *Poets* Justice) that they have not of late exposed any *Vice*, in the *Romish Priests* or *Turkish Mufti*, nor meddled with any of their Opinions. However, there may perhaps be a good Reason assign'd for it. They think their own Cause cannot do so well unless *Religion* is overturn'd. Now, Blessed be ve *God*, the greateſt Danger of our *Church* ſeems to come from theſe forreign Quarters, and therefore the *Poets* are cautious leſt they ſhould diſoblige their beſt Friends and Confederates.

The *Clergy* receiving their Education in the *Univerſities*, the *Poets* accordingly endeavour to vilify theſe Seminaries of Learning, and I wonder at their total Omiſſion of the Diſſenting Schools. The Univerſity of *Oxford* (e) made a Decree in *Convocation*, Anno 1584, againſt admitting *Stage Players* within their Juriſdiction, *leſt the Younger Sort ſhould be Spectators of ſo many lewd and evil Sports as are practiſed in them.* This Decree is never to be forgiven, becauſe it was never yet repealed. *The Stage Beaux toſs'd in a Blanket* (f) ſhews a poor Revenge upon a *Colledge Servitor*, but *An Act at Oxford* ſeems wholly deſigned to expoſe every Member from the Higheſt to the Loweſt. (g) Above twenty Inſtances may be produced from this very *Play.* 'Tis true the *Players* cared not to act it, and affront ſo great a Body in *Wholeſale*; the *Poet* therefore minces the Matter in another *Play* call'd *Hampſtead Heath*, where a great Part of theſe Inſolencies went off by *Retail*

(e) Dr. Reynolds *his* Overthrow of Stage Plays, *page* 152.

(f) *Page* 9, line penult.

(g) *Page* 2, *line* 18, 25 *and ult.* p. 3, l. 6. p. 4, l. 4, 13 *and* 27. p. 6. l. 10 and 29. p. 7, l. 25 *and* 30. p. 8, l. 12 p. 10, l. 4. p. 20, l. 20. p. 23, l. 19. p. 27, l. 30. p. 33, l. 31. p. 35. l. 32. p. 40, l. ult. p. 45, l. 29. p. 46, l. 6. p. 51, l. 6 and p. 55, l. 11.

with

with little Amendments. This *Play* was acted in *Drury-Lane*, and the *Actor's* Names may be seen in the *Drama*, who told the *Hearers*, That (h) a *Servitor's Business is to pimp for Gentlemen Commoners*, That they [i] are *wretched Scoundrels*, and *sorry Dogs*, That [k] the *Tutors* are *crabbed Fellows*, and only teach a *Parcel of crabbed Authors*, Nay, that [l] the *Doctors* themselves have *no Divinity*. In this Respect *The Female Wits*, acted in the same Place, and by the same Persons, shew as little Manners or Modesty; since one of them gives [m] her *Opinion of the University Students*, That they are commonly *slovenly Fellows*, without any *Ingenuity*, their *Provision* is very *wretched*, and their *Conversation* is no better; but yet they are *all proud*, *because they have been at Oxford*: And accordingly, *Oxford* is immediately censured, as a *Place*, 'fit only *to improve Beggars, and spoil Gentlemen; to make them vain, and think*, that *no Body hath Wit but themselves*.

(h) Page 12, line 14.

(i) Page 31, line 12.

(k) Page 1, line 12.

(l) Page 51, line 4.

(m) Page 7, line 3.

Had not the *Universities* been of the utmost Consequence, both to *Church* and *State*, and the Nurseries both for *Religion* and *Learning*, perhaps they

had

had not been so reflected on. However in *The Fair Example* there is [n]
as bold a Stroak, where one of the (n) Page 27, line 25,
Company is pleas'd to tell the Audience.

That he *maintains at present a matter of fifty sleeping Doctors in both Universities, that do nothing but dream.*
Had the *Players* brib'd any Members
of the *Universities* to espouse their Interest, they could but tell of it. However, their Reflections would be un-
grateful for what is past, and a small
Obligation for the Time to come.

The *Doctors* have Reason to beware
of shewing Encouragement to the *Actors*, least the *horrid Profaneness* of the
Stage should be interpreted as an Effect
of their being spoil'd at *Oxford*. Besides, what Favour they shew, may
be interpreted by the *Actors* as a Duty;
because they say, that the *Doctors* are
beholden to them for a Maintainance.
However, none but they can dare to
affront so venerable a Body, without
any Fear of a just Resentment. I
need not mention, what is said in o-
ther *Play-Houses*; this alone is sufficient.

The last Instance of their good
Breeding, their Manners, and fine
Language

(o) The British Enchanters, pa. 14, line penult.

(p) Love's Contrivance, printed 1703. pa. 16, line 3.

(q) An Act at Oxford, page 34, line ult. &c. Hampstead Heath, page 39, &c.

(r) As you find it, printed 1703, pa. 7, line 13 and 21. p. 9, l. 3 and 10. The Lawyer's Fortune, page 45, line 8. Signature, G 3. The Portsmouth Heiress, page 37, line

Language is known from their Treating of the *Ladies*. I have shewn already how they are adored with Expressions of *Rank Blasphemy*. It will therefore be necessary to observe the *Virtues* which render them so amiable. Now without any Ceremony, they are represented sometimes as (o) the worst of *Plagues* which can befall Mankind, sometimes as (p) horridly *false*, sometimes as (q) *impudent* in Courting of Men, but generally as (r) notorious *Whores*. This is the only Place where the *Ladies* will sit and hear themselves abus'd, under Pretence of Diversion. If the *Poet's* Studies are not near *Billingsgate*, yet certainly their Conversation lies chiefly among the *Oyster-Women*, and such as deserve the *Ducking Stool:* And since the *Actors* have no better *Manners*, the *Ladies* ought in Prudence to abstain from such Places, where they are so scandalously abused.

54, line 30. The Roving Husband reclaim'd page 37, line 17. Ulysses, page 13, line 29. p. 14, l. 22.

CHAP.

CHAP. IX.

The Stage a declared Enemy to all Reformation.

THE laſt Charge which I ſhall draw up againſt the *Stage* is their poſitive Declaring againſt all *Reformation* either in themſelves or others. This ſhews their Obſtinacy in the Higheſt Degree, and that tho' they pretend to be *Her Majeſties* Servants, nay, *Her* ſworn Servants; yet they defy *Her* Orders, and grow rather worſe than better, for *Her* pious Care and ſincere Endeavours to reclaim them. Here *Law* and *Divinity*, *Queen* and *Subject*, *Judge* and *Juries*, *Charges* and *Sermons*, *Lords* and *Commons*, *Magiſtrates* and *Clergy* are all valued alike. Let them endeavour to *reform* the World if they dare; they ſhall ſoon hear of it from the *Stage*, and be Affronted, Cenſur'd, Deſpis'd and Expos'd, and what is but whiſpered in other Places, is there ſhewn Bare-faced.

I ſuppoſe it is evident from the former *Chapters*, that the *Stage* is now as bad

N   as

as ever, and hates to be *reform'd*, that it is *obstinate* to the highest Degree, and abuseth all such who according to their several Offices, should be *a terror to evil doers*, and *a praise to them that do well :* But as the *Poets* and their Friends, usually cry out for farther Proof, so to gratify them, it will not be amiss to mention some other Particulars.

Mr *Collier* expos'd two *Plays* written by Mr. *Dennis*, call'd *The Relapse*, and *The Provok'd Wife*, and made good his Assertions in Opposition to the feeble Efforts of that *Author.* The *Actors* of *The Provok'd Wife* were afterward prosecuted at Law, found guilty, and fin'd for uttering several scandalous Expressions contained therein. This Usage would put any one, but a *Poet* out of Countenance, and yet Mr. *Dennis* glorying in his Shame, having afterward (*a*) The written (*a*) some other *Plays* little Confedera- better than the former, stiles himself in cy, *and* The the *Title Page*, *The Author* of these Mistake. scandalous *Comedies.*

Besides, The present Age is frequently derided by the *Actors*, because (blessed be *God*.) there are great Endeavours for a *Reformation* of Manners. Enough. of this *Language* may be seen

in

in (*b*) *Prologues* and *Epilogues* made for this Purpose, where the *Actors* address themselves to the *Pit*, and speak for the Information of the *Audience*. I shall only give the Reader a Taft hereof, from one of (*c*) their *Epilogues*.

(*b*) The Rival Brothers, *Prologue*. The FemaleWits *Prologue*

(*c*) The Stage Beaux tofs'd in a Blanket, *Epilogue, pa. 3, line* 7.

With Zeal and Sin at once we're ftrangely warm'd,
And grow more wicked, as we grow reform'd.
Oh! 'tis a bleffed Age, and bleffed Nation,
When Vice walks Cheek by Jole with Reformation.

Sometimes it is call'd in Derifion (*d*) a *Reforming Age*, and (*e*) a *Saintlike Age*. Our *Modern Societies* are defcrib'd as fuch who (*f*) *are not fincerely reform'd,* but endeavour to *mend others more than themfelves.* A modern *Reformer* is (*g*) one who *can fee other Mens Faults, better than his own.* He who is *zealous* to fupprefs *Profanenefs,* is ftil'd (*h*) *a Buftler for Reformation*; and 'tis well if (*i*) he efcapes without Cenfure. The Name of an *Informer* in

(*d*) The Rival Brothers, *Prologue line* 2. The Lawyers Fortune *page* 9, *line* 16.

(*e*) An Act at Oxford, *page* 8, *line* 22. Hampftead Heath, *page* 10, *line* 20.

(*f*) As you find it, *printed* 1703, *page* 67, *line* 22.

(*g*) The Portfmouth Heirefs, *page* 48, *line* 1.
(*h*) The Lawyers Fortune, *page* 19, *line* 10.
(*i*) The Quacks, *page* 15, *alias* 11, *line* 1.

N 2   the

(k) Love's Contrivance, printed 1703, pa. 12, line 18.

the (k) *Play-House Language* is as odious as those of *Traitor, Cheat, Knave, Coward, Rascal, Thief* and *Varlet.* Here we are told that (l) *in the crying*

(l) As you find it, printed 1703, page 32, line 24.

out against our Immoralities, the Accusers have nothing to brag of, but both Prisoners and Evidence are equally guilty. One tells us (m) that *if we reform and*

(m) The Confederacy, page 4, line 35.

live honest, it is way to be starv'd. Another *Principal Actor* in a *Play* hath a bold Stroak at large (n) *Religion! Ay,*

(n) The Portsmouth Heiress, pa. 6, line 9.

there's another Topick now. Religion and Reformation! Two things that make a mighty stir in the World, without any considerable Progress, preach'd up every where, and followed no where. 'Tis as easy to reform the Follies and Vices of the Age by scandal [i.e. by Preaching against *Vices,* and informing against Offenders] *as to perswade a Young Fellow of my Inches, that there's any thing in that Religion that reins him from his Pleasure.* That is in short, *Religion* is a Cheat, and *Reformation* is impossible. And lastly, Another hearing *Vice* reproved breaks

(o) Love at firstSight, page 14, line 21,

out into (o) this *Sarcastical* Expression. *O I'm sick, perfectly sick, out of Order! Did you observe that Religious Air with which she spoke?* And then proceeds with an Oath, *'Tis so unlike a Gentlewoman,*

that

that a Country Lady who had only been three short Minutes at Court, would be heartily ashamed to talk so, when she went down again to her Husband.

If then such must feel the *Poets* Lash, who endeavour to reform *Vice,* tho' they let the *Stage* alone, what Usage must such expect to attempt to reclaim the *Play-House?* They shall have Dirt enough cast at them, that some at least may stick, and whoever escapes, they have their Share. The *Comedy* call'd *The Stage Beaux toss'd in a Blanket,* is from the Beginning to the End on this Subject, and the *Epilogue* is very scandalous. Here Mr. *Collier* is censur'd, despis'd, brought in guilty of Whoredom, and makes a dishonourble *Exit.* I thought, that *Tossing in a Blanket* was an Office too mean for a *Poet;* however upon Occasion he can stoop so low, and accordingly he treats his Opponent more like a *Dog* than a *Christian,* that so the *Title-Page* and the *Play* may be both of a Piece. It is well, that the *Law* secures the *English Subjects,* and restrains the Malice of the *Poets;* but by this we may observe, what they would be at, if they had a *Power* proportionable to their *Inclination.*

N 3   The

The *Abusing* the *Reformers* of the *Stage* is now a new Subject, to employ the *Poet's* Wit and Spleen ; and, I confess, is a very odd one for *Her Majesties* sworn Servants to speak, since she her self is one of the Number : But no matter for that, if she will put the *Poets* out of their old Road, she must expect her Share among the Rest.

(q) An Act at Oxford, *Epist. Dedicatory. page* 4, &c.

Sometimes they reflect on the *Reformers* of the *Stage* in their *Epistles, Dedicatory* and *Prefaces*, as (q) Enemies to the *Church* and *present Government*,

(r) *Zelmane, Epist. Dedicatory, page* 1, line 7, &c.

and as (r) *snarling Zealots* ; and tell us that (s) now the *Liberty of the Stage declines* [so much the better] and that

(s) The Portsmouth Heiress, *Preface, line* 3, &c.

Plays, as tho they were not dull enough before, must now, to oblige the affected Zeal and Humour of some Kind of People, be robb'd of all the Life and* Pertness [that is the Blasphemy and Profaneness] *which is in them.*

(t) The Gamester, pa. 6. line 16.
(u) Ibid.
(x) The Stage Beaux

They tell us also in their *Acts*, that such who oppose them (t) do *rail,* they are (u) *Whigs*, they are (x) an *Hypocritical Party*, nay, (y) *Inveterate Hypocrites*, who are Enemies to the

toss'd in a Blanket, *Title page. page* 43, *line* 18. *p.* 58, *l.* 29. *p.* 59, *l.* 2.
(y) The Stage Beaux toss'd in a Blanket, *page* 49, *line* 17.

Stage,

Stage, and say that (*z*) *if the Stage did not make it it's Business to expose Knaves and Hypocrites, they would say nothing against it.* (*a*) *Do you think* [saith one concerning Mr. Collier] *that any Man alive could say so many severe things against both Sexes, without having a sufficient Experience of those Evils and Frailties in himself?* They represent such as (*b*) guilty of *Whoring,* and tell them (*c*) *that if they are such Zealots for Morality, they should first reform themselves.* In their Censures they have no Regard to Truth or Equity ; if they can render such Persons despicable, it is no Matter how they effect it ; and it is observable that these Reflections may with equal Force be applied to the Preaching of the Word, and all Instructions in *Religion* ; and indeed if *Stage Poets* had their Wills, I doubt all would fare alike. In their *Prologues* and *Epilogues* they are sometimes (*d*) wholly on this Subject, when they speak more particularly to the Audience. There is one Quotation which I shall venture to transcribe, for the sake of the *Excellent English,* and *smooth Running* of the Verse which is almost as remarkable as the (*e*) *Poets* Scurrility.

(*z*) The Stage Beaux toss'd in a Blanket, *page* 50 *line* 9

(*a*) The Stage Beaux toss'd in a Blanket, *page* 57, *line* 14.

(*b*) The Stage Beaux toss'd in a Blanket, *page* 55, *line* 29. *to the End of the Play.*

(*c*) The Stage Beaux toss'd in a Blanket, *page* 49, *line* 18.

(*d*) The Faithful General, *Prologue* The Rival Brothers, *Prologue.* The Female Wits, *Prologue.* The Stage Beaux toss'd in a Blanket, *Epilogue.*

(*e*) The Faithful Bride of Granada, *Epilogue line* 3.

Sure

Sure we've scap'd the Informers Inqui-
    sition;
The Disease is bad, and he a damn'd Phy-
    sitian:
Him no Motive do's to Reformation lead
But Want, he swears because it get's him
    Bread.
He culls the Ill, and earns from thence
    his Food;
He, with Mending, he's ruin'd if the
    World is good.
No, great Examples shall reform the Stage.
Must we learn Manners from the vilest
    of the Age?

Had this came from a *School-Boy*
it would have deserv'd Correction; but
as it comes from a *Stage-Poet*, it is
very fine, and deserves a *Plaudite*. It
is abusive, and therefore excellent. I
have heard of some *Children*, who learn
to curse, before they can speak plain,
and the *Poet* writes scurrilously, when
he cannot write Sense. Had he been a
Child, he might have learn'd better
Manners; but as he is old, I doubt
it will be the more difficult to reclaim him.

(f) The
Faithful Gene-
ral, Prologue,
line L.
Thus we see that they spare neither
Writers nor *Reformers*, (f) such *Thought-*
    less

less Criticks of the Age, as they term them. Sometimes they have a Fling (g) at them, and away again to another Subject, and sometimes they ridicule both them and the Preaching of the Word of *God* together, as if both were alike Enemies to the *Stage* ; and from thence we may explain their *Arguments with a double Entendre.* Some Instances of this Nature may bear a publick View, and therefore let the *Reader* judge of them.

(*g*) The Careless Husband, *page 53, line* 10. Squire Trelooby, *Prologue, line* 22. The Biter, *Epilogue line* 24 *and in the End.* The Gamester, *page 6, line 16.* The Stage Coach, *Epilogue, line 7.* Zelmane, *Preface, page 1, line 8.*

Squire Trelooby, *Prologue line* 3.

To th' Stage the Army of Reformers come,
Sworn Foes to Wit as Carthage *was to*
  Rome:
Their Ears so sanctify'd no Scenes can please,
But heavy Hymns, and pensive Homilies.

Ibid. line 17.

With Force and fitting Freedom Vice ar
  raign,
Tho' Pulpits flatter, let the Stage speak
  plain.

It will not be omiss to give the *Reader* a Taft of their *Fine Language* in Profe as well as Verfe, and becaufe I
                                    will

will not tire him with many Quotations, I shall mention only a few taken out of *The Stage Beaux toss'd in a Blanket.* The *Author* begins very roundly in (*b*) the *Epistle Dedicatory*; and tells us, that *the Stage hath no Enemies, but such as are Hypocrites, and real Enemies to Virtue,* and gives this Reason, *Because the Stage is a professed Enemy to them and their darling Vices.* This is a bold Assertion; and the Falshood is as evident as the Enmity. However there is much more to the same Purpose, in the *Play* it self.

(*b*) Page 2, line 18.

Page 29, line 8.

An Opposer of the *Stage* is call'd *A Man of loose Principles, who can be guilty of arrogating to himself a Righteousness above all Men, as well as a Judgment and Sense superiour to all the Men of Wit in Town.*

Page 2, line 37.

They ought to abhor the Play-House, since they so often see their ugly Faces there.

Ibid. line 39.

The Stage-Glass is not made to flatter Fools and Knaves, and therefore they and
their

their Friends are for Breaking the honest Mirrour.

Ibid. line penult.

Fools and Knaves have a real Quarrel with the Stage, not that it shews their Pictures deformed to themselves, but to every Body else.

Page 3, line 4.

The greatest Pique Men have to the Stage is, because their Follies and Vices are too conspicuous, and too well belov'd.

Page 58, line 29. spoken by an Enemy of the Stage, endeavouring to debauch a Woman of the same Temper.

Put off the Veil, I know you are an Hypocrite. [Answer] *Nay, Now you begin to be abusive. An Hypocrite!* [Reply] *Nay, I am sure of it, for almost all our Party are so.*

But an *Actor* tells us, (i) that *now Vice may go on and prosper: The Stage dares hardly shew a vicious Person speaking like himself, for fear of being call'd profane, for exposing him.* And to this another answers, *'Tis hard indeed when*

(i) The Careless Husband, page 53, line 10.

People

People won't diftinguish between what's meant for Contempt, and what for Example.

Is there then no Curb to *Vice* except the *Stage*? Do the *Scriptures* the Ordinances of *God*, and *Laws* of the Land fignify nothing in this Cafe? Thefe are infignificant in their Efteem, and they had much rather that thefe fhould be abolifhed, than that the *Play-Houfe* fhould be under Correction. But is the *Stage afraid to fhew a vicious Perfon fpeaking like himfelf?* To what height of Impiety would they then arrive, if they had their Will? Are not their vicious Perfons reprefented on the *Stage*? Do they not fpeak like themfelves? Do they not contemn *God* and *Religion*? Do they not belch out moft dreadful *Oaths* and *Curfes*? And yet they would do worfe if they dared. However, all vicious Expreffions are not fit to be reprefented. Whatever is a *Sin* when fpoken in another Place, is as much a *Sin* when fpoken in the *Play-Houfe*. If we are willing to expofe a vicious Expreffion, it is better to make a Report thereof as fpoken by another, and then refent it accordingly. I doubt not but if *Horace* was alive he
                                    would

would fay of our Expreſſions, as he ſaid of other Repreſentations *(k)* That they are not fit to come without the *Scenes.* However, I am ſure that the *Scriptures* condemn ſuch things in general. We are there cautioned *(l)* not to *ſwear* or *blaſpheme* at all, that *no corrupt communication ſhould proceed out of our mouths,* and that ſuch *things ſhould not be once named* among us, and I am ſure that the *Stage* hath no particular Diſpenſation. The Word of *God* ſhall regulate their Sayings when they pleaſe, but not upon the *Stage.* I know not which is the worſt either the *Sin* or the *Apology.*

Is it *hard when People won't diſtinguiſh between what's meant for Contempt, and what for Example?* 'Tis as hard that the *Poets* will not write ſo, as that it may be diſtinguiſhed. When the *Gentlemen* of the chief *Character* in the *Play* talk atheiſtically, and profane, and are rewarded with Succeſs, this muſt be interpreted as meant for Contempt. When *Women* of a principal Character *ſwear, curſe, blaſpheme* and talk *Smut,* this muſt be meant for *Contempt.* It is indeed a Contempt to the *Sex,* but rather a Credit ſhewn to the *Vice.* But ſuppoſe they are reprov'd. What then?

(k) Lib. de Arte Poetica.

Non tamen intus Digna geri promes in Scenam multaq; tolles.

(l) Matth. 5. 34, 35, 36, 37. Jam. 5. 12. 1 Tim. 1. 20. Eph. 4. 29, 30 and 5. 3, 4, 5, 6, 7.

If

If one Man sins, and another reproves him for it, doth this take off the Guilt, and make it no *Sin* in the Sight of God? One Man injures his Neighbour, and another blames him for it; doth this cancel the Guilt, and make the Fact nothing? One Man speaks *Blasphemy*, and another reproves him; doth this justify the Boldness? or make the Words unspoken? This is a cheap Way of atoning for past Offences, and how it will make Amends, I cannot imagine. However, most of the Vicious Expressions spoken on the *Stage*, are spoken without any Reproof at all. Sometimes the Reprover is at the same Time guilty of the Crime, which he reproves, as particularly in (*m*) the Case of *Swearing*. At another Time (*n*) the *Reproofs* are ridicul'd, and the *Reprover* out of Countenance; and it is as observable, that (*o*) the Profane Person goes on in the same Course to the End of the *Play* without Amendment, and those, who reproved at first, have afterwards shewn themselves reconciled and pleased with all the past Behaviour; and a Concern for *horrid Impieties* is (*p*) shewn only by *taking the name of God in vain.* These are the *Methods* of the

Play

(*m*) **Love at first Sight,** *page 66, line 24.*

(*n*) **Love at first Sight,** *page 14, line 21.*

(*o*) **The Confederacy,** *page 13, line 8, &c. page 32 and 33. p.71, l. 5, &c. and p. 72, l. 1 and 21.*

(*p*) **The Mistake,** *pa. 49. Sheet I line 17 & 21.*

Play-House in reproving of *Vice*, insomuch that it is evident from their whole Conduct, that they only encourage the *Sin*, and shame the *Reprover*.

It is therefore the greatest Jest of all, That when the *Stage* is tax'd with *Swearing*, *Cursing*, *Blasphemy*, and all Manner of *Profaneness*, and the *Poets* are called upon to mend their Manners, they tell us, that (*q*) they are the true *Reformers* of the Nation, they arraign and condemn *Vice*, their Design is to *reform* our Minds, and regulate our Morals. Indeed, I hardly thought, until I read it, that they had Confidence enough for such an Assertion, especially after all the Efforts in Print, to convince the World of their *horrid Impieties*. Perhaps in the Devil's *Chappels*, they use the Words *Virtue*, *Religion* and *Reformation*, to signify such things as please him best : and the Words *Vice* and *Hypocrisy* for something which is contrary to his Interest. If they take them in their common Acceptation, 'tis too late to use this Plea. The Nation is convinc'd already, and know what they aim at, and such a Vindication of their Behaviour shews, that they are resolved to

(*q*) An Act at Oxford, *Preface* page 5. Hampstead Heath, *Prologue line* 11. The Biter, *Epilogue line* 13 *and penult*. The Careless Husband, *page* 53, *line* 10.

go on in their old Course. Do their horrid *Oaths* and *Curses* tend to a *Reformation?* Are their *Exposing* of *Virtue*, *Encouraging* of *Vice*, *Affronting* of *God*, and *Adoring* of the *Devil*, Signs of *Reformation?* This the Players feem to affert with all the Affurance imaginable. The *Reformation* which they drive at, is to reduce us from *Christianity* to *Paganism*, or rather from *Religion* to *Atheism*. Had they therefore been filent, and endeavour'd to amend their Faults, it had been but common Prudence to themfelves and their Caufe, and many would have put a favourable Conftruction thereon; but fince they thus vindicate themfelves, it is too fad a Sign, that they are given over to a *Reprobate Senfe*, and that nothing, but their total Suppreffion, can hinder that Deluge of *Impiety*, which they ftrive to bring upon us, with the Pretence of *Reformation*. Never fince the *Creation* of the World, was *God* fo vifibly affronted as on the *Stage*. Never was the *Devil* fo publickly ador'd in a *Criftian Nation* as on the *Stage*. Never was *Religion* fo openly undermin'd, as on the *Stage*. Never were the *Doctines* of *Chriftianity* fo mifapplied as on the *Stage*. Never were *Supe-*

riors

riors so affronted, without a due Resentment, as upon the *Stage* ; and yet they pretend to be the only *Persons* to *reform* the World, and that without their Assistance, *Vice* will go on and prosper. They tell us that the *Pulpits flatter, whilst the Stage speaks plain.* I think the *Pulpits* never flatter'd them, and I hope, never will. The *Poets* render all others, who endeavour a *Reformation,* as the greatest *Sinners,* and grossest *Hypocrites* in Nature. These Men would make excellent Soldiers, since the Brass which they carry, would be Proof against a Cannon Bullet. It is a Sign, that their Cause wants a Support, when they have recourse to such evident Lies ; and unless by a *Reformation* they intend to destroy the Principles of Good and Evil, and introduce *Atheism* with all manner of *Licentiousness,* it is plain, that what they plead for themselves, is the most notorious Falshood which ever was urged with the like Confidence. Had they pleaded guilty, they might have deserved Favour ; but since they justify themselves in such a Manner, they justly, when convicted, deserve the highest Censure.

O   CHAP.

CHAP. X.

The Conclusion.

FROM what hath been said in the former Chapters, it evidently appears, That the *horrid Licentiousness* of the *English Stage*, its *Profaneness*, *Immorality* and *filthy Expressions* do far exceed the worst, which are to be found not only in all the Christian, but even in *Heathen Countries*. Whilst we are reform'd from the *Church of Rome*, our *Comedies* are a Scandal to our Reformation, and we may say to our Shame of *France*, *Spain* and *Italy*, as the Prophet *Ezekiel*, (a) formerly said of *Samaria* and *Sodom*; *They have not done*, in this Respect, *as we have done; they have not committed half our Sins, but we have multiplied our abominations more than they.* The lewd Expressions of the Actors are as flaming as ever. They rail at *Virtue*, and speak well of *Vice*. They discountenance *Religion*, and encourage *Profaneness*. They defy even *God* himself, and laugh at the Endeavours us'd by

Man

(a) *Chap.* 16. 48, 51.

Man for their *Reformation.* Thefe things are the Subject of their Scorn and Contempt, their Sport and Paftime? and thus they have rendered the Attempts to reclaim them ineffectual. The *Theatres* are the *Synagogues* of *Satan.* Their *Votaries* feem rampantly bold in Sin, and openly addicted to the Service of the *Devil.* The *Plays* are a chief Caufe of the *Vices* of the Age, and the *bitter root that brings forth gall and wormwood.* They fhew to the World many dreadful Examples of all Sorts of *Impiety,* and expofe *Vice* (as they tell us) not for Reproof, but for Imitation; not to fupprefs it, but to increafe the Fafhion. *Profanenefs* is the chief Commodity in which they deal, and therefore they expofe it, like *Merchants* and Tradefmen, to promote the Sale, and difperfe it through the Nation. Our *Poets* (b) feem now more than ever, to fence againft Cenfure, by the Excefs of *Profanenefs,* and to make the overgrown Size of their Crimes a Ground for Impunity. Their monftrous *Impieties* are almoft too big to be throughly view'd, and too fhameful to bear a Tryal. *David* feems fitly to defcribe them; (c) They are

(b) Collier's *Short View of the Stage,* Page 179.

(e) 2 *Sam.* 23. 6, 7.

O 2

are as thorns thrust away, Because they can-
not be taken with hands. But the man that
shall touch them, must be fenced with
iron, and the staff of a spear. They
are so fortified with *Smut*, and deeply
intrench'd in *Nastiness*, that where they
deserve most, there is no Coming at
them. Many of their Expressions are
too dreadful to be related, insomuch
that the bare Repeating of them hath
been thought of dangerous Consequence,
and a Means to spread the Infection;
and yet they are too scandalous to be
conceal'd, lest an universal Silence
should be constru'd as an Approbation,
contract a publick Guilt, and bring
upon us a publick Calamity. The *hor-*
rid Oaths and *Curses,* so frequently
heard, might have been suppress'd before this Time, by the due Execution
of the Laws, at least new ones had
not been invented, if the *Stage* had not
continually refreshed the Memory of
the *Hearers,* and harden'd them in *Sin,*
by such dreadful Examples.

The very *Fable* of the *Plays* are oftentimes scandalously immodest; and
what they call the *Moral,* teacheth *Immo-*
rality. The whole Plot of the *Poet* is employ'd this Way, and all the Inferences
which

which can be made from their Manner of Conversation, are *vicious* and *profane.* These things can scarcely be discovered, but by a Multiplicity of Words, and Dissecting of whole *Plays.* The *Poets* think, that no one will take the Pains to discover these Mysteries, and this makes them the bolder in such Representations. To be short, The Conduct of *Constant* and *Lady Brute* in the *Provok'd Wife* teacheth us, that if the Husband is unkind, the Wife ought in Revenge to play the Whore, and the Man, who commits Adultery with her, is to be commended for his Constancy, if he was once a Suitor. In *the Roving Husband Reclaim'd*, the *Colonel*, the *Lady of Quality*, Mrs. *Politick*, Mrs. *Venture* and the *Conjurer* attack *Fidelia* in the same Manner, and their Conversation of this Kind is enough to make any Woman asham'd, except a S*tage-frequenter.* The Success of *Valere* in the *Gamester*, and *The Lady Reveller* in the Basset Table commends the *Vices* which they would seem to oppose. The *Play* call'd *Solon* is a Satyr upon *Philosophy*, not only in the Person of *Cleanthus*, but also in *Solon* himself, whose *Laws* are

O 3   expos'd,

expos'd, who sinks beneath his Character, is foolishly in Love, and in the Conclusion declares against *Morality*. The *Portsmouth-Heiress* hath a general Compound of *Vice*, and every Debauchee is crown'd with Success. *Gibraltar* and *Love at first Sight* are but little better. The *Play* call'd *an Act at Oxfird* strangely vilifies the *Universities* in every Particular, and a great Part of the Scurrility is afterward repeated in *Hampstead-Heath*. *The Faithful General* will teach us to worship *Pagan Idols*, *The British Enchanters* will teach us to adore the *Devil*, and we may learn an *Hymn* to his *Praise and Glory* out of *The Metamorphosis*. *The Confederacy* teacheth a *Master* to employ his *Man* in all wicked Designs, and teacheth the *Man* to deny Matter of Fact, with all imaginable Impudence, and what is wanting herein to compleat a *Monster of Iniquity*, may be learn'd in *Love the Leveller* from the *Priests of Isis*.

Besides, it is as certain, that if any of our former Performances are worse than the rest, they are the Darlings of the present *Stage*, and acted there, either to keep the later *Poets* in Countenance,

tenance, or as Patterns for them to exceed. There are but three *Plays* lately reprinted, *viz. The Northern Lass, The Loyal Subject* and *The Royal Merchant.* The first was written in the Time of *Ben. Johnson,* and the other two by *Beaumont* and *Fletcher.* Our *Muses* were then comparatively inoffensive, and are therefore generally neglected. But these *Plays* which are selected from the rest, are remarkably scandalous for (*d*) *Swearing* (*e*) *Cursing,* (*f*) *Smut* and *Profaneness,* in making a Jest of (*g*) the *Devil,* (*h*) the Torments of *Hell,* and (*i*) the Joys of

(*d*) The Northern Lass, page 1, line 5. and 7. p. 3. l. 29. p. 4. l. 8. p. 5. l. 10. p. 6. l. 30. p. 7. l. 25. p. 8. l. 2. p. 16 l. 33. p. 17. l. 12. p. 19. l. 7. p. 20. l. 27. p. 23. l. 20. p. 27. l. 36. p. 36. l. 33. p. 39. l. 21. p. 41. l. 29. p. 54. l. ult. p. 56. l. 18. p. 59. l. 18. and p. 60. l. 1, 3 and 15. The Loyal Subject, page 27. line 16 and 29. p. 29. l. 18. p. 31. l. 40. p. 43. l. 5 and 15. p. 44. l. 35. p. 47. l. 38. p. 48. l. 7. p. 53. l. 4 and 11. p. 66. l. 29 and 35. and p. 69. l. 34. The Royal Merchant, page 12. line 5. p. 26. l. 32. p. 29. l. 25. p. 35. l. 6. and 20. p. 48. l. 21. p. 51. l. 4 and 15. p. 54. l. 13. p. 57. l. 27. p. 58. l. 12. p. 59. l. 18. and p. 71. l. 27 and 28.

(*e*) The Northern Lass, page 4. line 16. and p. 57. l. 20. The Loyal Subject, page 4. line 35. p. 12. l. 32, to the End. and p. 13. l. 1, to 17. p. 39, l. 42. p. 57. l. 28. and p. 73. l. 30. The Royal Merchant, page 49. line 6. p. 55. l. 27. and p. 56. l. 23.

(*f*) The Northern Lass, Prologue, line 20. Epilogue, line 23. page 3. line 21. Sheet E p 24. l. 26. p. 39. l. 34. p. 40. l. 12. p. 44. l. antepenult. p. 55. l. 13. p. 65. l. 17. and p. 66. l. 4. The Loyal Subject, page 45. line 20. p. 47. l. 12. The Royal Merchant, page 28. line antepenult. p. 30. l. 29.

(*g*) The Northern Lass, page 40. line 5. The Royal Merchant, page 29. line 9.

(*h*) The Loyal Subject, page 31. line 40.

(*i*) The Loyal Subject, page 44. line 13.

O 4   *Heaven:*

Heaven; besides the Expoſing of (k) Magiſtrates and (l) Conſtables, and Ridiculing the (m) Notion of Divine Illumination. Our Actors might have found much better Plays in the antient Authors; but perhaps, ſuch might ſhame our preſent Poets, or diſoblige their Hearers.

Neither do they take only the worſt of our antient Poetry, but alſo the Dregs of forreign Countries. Molier could afford us from France ſuch Plays as are built upon a Moral Foundation; but when a Part of his Works are tranſlated for our Diverſion, it muſt be either The Metamorphoſis, where (n) the Devil is ſcandalouſly ador'd, or Squire Trelooby, which at beſt, is good for nothing: And left theſe Diſhes ſhould not pleaſe the Engliſh Palate, the Tranſlator takes Care to ſet them off with all the Advantages of (o) Swearing, (p) Curſing, (q) Invoking of

(n) Page 14.

(o) Squire Trelooby, page 5. line 8. p. 8. l. 4, and 24. p. 11 l. antepenult. p. 13. l. 16. p. 39. l. 16. and ult. p. 49. l. 14. and 25. p. 52. l. 1. and 11. The Metamorphoſis, page 29. line antepenult. p. 31. line 12. p. 36, l. 16. p 40. l. 4 p. 51. l. 5.

the

the **Devil**, and (*r*) *Adjuring* in his Name, (*s*) *Calling* upon *God* on ridiculous Occasions, and *Trifling* with (*t*) their Hopes of *Salvation*, and (*u*) the *Truth* of the *Gospel*, and (*x*) where the *Translator* had the Liberty to speak his own Sense, he largely exposes *Religion* and *Reformation*, the *Clergy* and *Societies*.

(*r*) Squire Trelooby, *page* 22. *line* 8. *p.* 38. *l.* 23.

(*s*) Squire Trelooby, *page* 20. *line* 1. *and antepenult.*

(*t*) Squire Trelooby, *page* 11. *line* 11.

(*u*) Squire Trelooby, *page* 40. *line* 17.

(*x*) Squire Trelooby, *Prologue and Epilogue.*

The Expressions in the *Italian Opera* call'd *The Temple of Love*, are inoffensive throughout, because the *Translator* (*y*) was confin'd to the same Number of *Syllables* which were in the *Original*; but left there should be nothing to please the Humour of the Age, he inserts in (*z*) the *Epilogue* an *Oath*, by the *Death of God.*

(*y*) *Title Page, line* 5.

(*z*) *Line* 3.

Thus we see that our *Plays* are now grown to such an Height of *Profaneness*, that it is really a Penance for Good Men to read them, and offensive to all *Christians* to hear them. They sometimes chill the Blood, and must either fear the *Conscience*, or raise an *Abhorrene*. The Poets, like (*a*) *evil men and seducers wax worse and worse, deceiving and being deceived.*

(*a*) 2 *Tim.* 3. 13.

They,

They have so far prevailed, in infecting Men's Minds, that there is now no Relish for any *Poetry*, but what is Scurrilous, Smutty, Immoral, Blasphemous and Profane. In this alone their Wit is shewn, and for this alone they are generally admired. If an English *Play* is less Scandalous than the Rest, it is rejected as dull and tedious; but if it bids Defiance to both *God* and *Man* it is admired for its Life and Pertness. In the *Play-House* at the *Hay Market* there was only a Pretence of *Reformation*, but it prov'd so fatal, that the Undertakers were forc'd to desist, and have at their Cost shewn to the World, that even such a Pretence will ruin their Interest. The *Tragedy* call'd *Liberty Asserted*, had in the Main a good Design, *viz.* to expose the *French Tyranny*, and commend the *English Constitution*; but it met with such bad Success, that the *Poet* was oblig'd to vindicate himself in the *Preface*; and this so prejudiced the *Hearers*, that his following *Play* call'd *Gibraltar*, tho, of a contrary Nature, shar'd in the same Fate, and (a) had put the *Poet* out of Countenance, only he was supported by the Example of *Terence*, who

(a) See the Preface.

who ſtood to it, that one of his *Plays* was good, when all the World condemn'd it. However this *Gentleman* is now forc'd to write like the reſt of his Brethren, and to ſupport his Credit, he afterwards ſtiles himſelf (*b*) the *Author* of *The Relapſe,* and *The Provok'd Wife,* two *Plays* which were horridly Scandalous, and conſequently the fitteſt to regain his Credit with the *Stage.* Neither was this the Fate of one Attempt of *Reforming Plays,* but others of the ſame Nature have had the ſame Misfortune. *The Lying Lover* is quite laid aſide. *The Gameſter* and *The Baſſet Table* are very rarely acted; and as there only ſeem'd to be a Deſign in them to *reform* theſe *Vices,* it was ſo fatal, that the ſcandalous Expreſſions in the *Plays* could not make Amends for ſo great a Miſmanagement, and none of them could bear a Second Edition. On the Contrary, (*c*) the moſt Scandalous *Plays* are moſt frequently reprinted, and (*d*) *The Recruiting Officer* already bears a Second Edition. *The Britiſh Enchanters* was frequently acted, and the *Blaſphemy* contain'd therein conſtantly made a full Houſe, and had not the *Devil* been actually

(*b*) Title Page of The Miſtake, *and* The Confederacy.

(*c*) The NorthernLaſs, *the 6th Impreſſion,* 1706. Love for Love, *the 4th Impreſſion,* 1704. The Spaniſh Fryar, *the 2d Edition,* 1704. The Provok'd Wife, *reprinted* 1698. Sir Courtly Nice, *mentioned in* A Repreſentation of the Impiety and Immorality of the Engliſh Stage, *page* 10, *Reprinted* 1703.

(*d*) *Printed in* March laſt, *and reprinted in* July.

actually ador'd his *Temple* had not at
that Time been so Scandalously frequented.   The horrid Comedies of *Love
for Love*, *The provok'd Wife*, and *The
Spanish Fryar*, are frequently acted in
all Places to which the *Players* come.
The more they have been expos'd by
Mr. *Collier* and (*e*) others, the more
they seem to be admir'd ; and this may
be the Reason of their frequent Pub-
lications from the Press as well as
from the *Stage*.   It is therefore too
evident, that the *Play-House* Interest
consists in promoting of *Vice*, and it
cannot be reform'd, but the *Actors* must
be ruin'd .   Accordingly we find by
sad Experience, that *Her Majesty's* pious Attempts, and the Endeavours of
others are unsuccesful, and how then
can we expect to have a greater Influence upon them ? Should they be re-
formed a little while, for Fear of
Shame and Punishment, yet this Fear
will soon be over, and when once they
think, that they can sin securely, they will
return to their former *Vomit*, *and wal-
low in the* beloved *Mire*.   The Time
was when the *English Stage* dared not
to *blaspheme*, but now it is their frequent *Language*, and the longer they
are

(*e*) A Repre-
sentation of
the Impiety
and Immorali-
ty of the Eng-
lish Stage.
page 7.

are tolerated, the more they are guilty. Their *Methods* have so justly provok'd all, who have a *Zeal* for *God*, and *Love* for *Religion*, that they reckon it a *Scandal* to be seen in such a Place. The *Hearers* therefore are Persons of a different Character. and such who are chiefly delighted with *Profaneness* and *Impiety*. The *Poets* and *Actors* know, that if they should *reform* their *Plays*, they should disoblige their *Hearers*, and then the Hopes of their Gains would be gone; and for this Reason, like *Demetrius*, they exclaim against it. So that since Reason and Experience shews us the Impossibility that they should be *reform'd*, it is high Time that they should be *Suppress'd.*

This was the Case at *Athens*, where the *Stage* began. At first it met with all possible Encouragement, and a vast Fund was settled for its Maintainance, which (*f*) our present *Poets* often glory in. This so exhausted their Treasure, that (*g*) they had no Mony to set forth their Ships, or defend their Country; and by this Means their Enemies prevail'd against them. When the *Athenian Stage* was offensive, they appointed

(*f*) Liberty Asserted, *Preface, line* 1. The Basset Table, *Dedication, line* 4. The Stage Beaux toss'd in a Blanket, *Dedication line* 4. (*g*) Plutarch *de Gloria Atheniensium*

appointed several Inspectors for its better Regulation. When this did not succeed, they passed a farther Censure, and made a Law, that (*h*) no *Magistrate*, or Judge of the *Areopagus*, should make a *Comedy*, because it was a disreputable Employment, and at last they (*i*) enacted, that Common *Actors* should from that Time be reputed infamous. Nay, *Horace* also observes, that (*k*) when the antient *Comedy* succeeded the *Tragick Poets*, they took too great a Liberty, insomuch that a Law was made against them, and accordingly they were suppress'd, when they were not able to be abusive any longer.

(*b*) Plutarch *ibid.*

(*i*) Chrysostomi *Hom.* 13, *in* 1 *Cor.* 4. *Tom.* 10.

(*k*) Horat. *de Arte* Poetica.
Successit vetus his Comœdiæ, non sine multâ
Laude ; sed in vitium libertas excidit, & vim
Dignam lege regi: Lex est accepta, Chorusq;
Turpiter obticuit, sublato jure nocendi.

The Antient *Romans*, whose Encouragement of the *Stage* is also (*l*) much boasted of, made a very early Law against them, in which they made them infamous, and ordain'd that none should be admitted to Court, the Bar, or the Senate, but should also be uncapable of

(*l*) Ulysses, Dedication, *pa.* 2, *line* 4. Zelmane, Dedication, *line* 10.

of any Military or other Honour and Esteem ; all which *Tertullian* recites, and then(*m*) asks this Question, *What a Confession is this, that these Things are e-vil; since the Actors, when they were in the greatest Esteem, were thus branded with a Mark of Disgrace ?* And I cannot but think, it is as great an Argument of a bad Cause, when its Abettors urge such Scraps of Stories to support it, which when truly related, are so full against it. Besides, these are all *Pagan* Instances. The *Greeks* and *Romans* were without *God* and his *Laws* : They were (*n*) *afar off,* they were *aliens to the common-wealth of Israel, and strangers from the covenant of promise, having no hope,* and Αθεοι, Atheists, or *without God in the world;* they were such Men, who (*o*) *did not like to retain God in their knowledge,* and *therefore God gave them over to a reprobate mind, to do those things which are not convenient.* These are the Countries, where the *Devil ruled among the children of disobedience.* These are the Places where he gene-rally deluded the People from his Oracles, returned Answers to such as came to enquire of him, and directed them,

(*m*) Lib. De Specta-culis, *page* 699, Edit. Basil. 1562.

(*n*) Eph. 2. 12, 13.

(*o*) Rom. 1. 23.

them, according as he thought moſt convenient for his own Intereſt: And therefore we need not be proud of *Plays*, becauſe they were invented in *Greece*, and promoted at *Rome*.

To theſe *Pagan* Examples I ſhall add others, which I take to be more material, and do accordingly affirm, That in all thoſe Countries, where the *Patriarchs* travailed, and where *God* revealed his will, either by *him-ſelf*, his *Angels* or his *Prophets*, and in all thoſe Countries, where the Iſraelites ſojourned, as well as in the Land of *Canaan*, where they afterward lived, there was no ſuch thing either known, or perhaps ſo much as talk'd of. For this Reaſon, there is no Word either in the *Hebrew* or *Chaldee* Languages, to ſignify a *Comedy* or a *Tragedy.* The Words alſo in (*p*) *Arabick* are evidently of a *Greek* Derivation, which were borrowed from thence in after Ages, and (*q*) an *Eaſtern Hiſtorian* tells us, that theſe Kinds of Poetry *were invented in* Theſſaly, which is a Part of *Greece.* Nay, when the *Jews* had altered their Language into the *Syriack*, by a Mixture of *Chaldee* and *Greek*, occaſioned by their

(*p*) קומידיא‎ Κωμωδία. טראגידיא‎ Τεαγωδία.
(*g*) Abu'l Pharagij, Hiſtoria Dynaſtarum *pag.* 33.

their Captivity in one Nation, and their Commerce with the other, even then the Name of a *Comedy* was so odious, that the very (r) Word was used, at that Time, only to signify a Curse, Disparagement and a Reproach. When (s) a Place of Exercise was first built in *Judea*, to introduce only the *Grecian Games*, it usher'd in a Contempt of *Religion*, a Neglect of the *Sacrifices*, and many other Calamities; and the Reason is mentioned. *For it is not a light thing to do wickedly against the law of God.* When *Herod* built a *Theatre* within *Jerusalem*, about thirty years before the Birth of *Christ*, (t) the *Jews* interrupted it, as a manifest Corruption of those Disciplines and Manners, which they had entertained and honoured among them; and accordingly it was opposed with the greatest *Zeal* and *Indignation. For (faith Josephus) it was an Impious thing to change and profane the Ordinances of the Country for Foreign Exercises.*

Neither was this *Zeal* only in the Time of the *Law*, but it rather increased under the *Gospel*. The *Primitive Christians* did not frequent the

(r) קומדיא

(s) 1 *Maccab.* 1. 11, 12, 13, 14, and 2 *Maccab.* 4. 7 to 18.

(t) Josephus Jewish Antiquities, Book 15, Chap. 11. *These two Quotations, from the Maccabees and Josephus are so full, that the Reader is desired to peruse them at large.*

P   Shews,

Shews which were made for the Entertainment of the People. They look'd upon the Publick Sports and Pastimes of those Days, (*u*) as the *Scenes* not only of *Folly* and *Lewdness*, but of great *Impiety* and *Idolatry*, as Places, where the *Devil* eminently rul'd, and reckon'd all his *Votaries*, who went thither. Their Abstaining from the *Stage* was so evident, that the *Heathen* in (*x*) *Minucius Falix* roundly charges them with it, and reckons it as a Crime, which when *Octavius* the *Christian* answers, he (*y*) owns the *Charge*, but denies the *Guilt*, and tells him, that there was good Reason to abstain from such *Shews*, *Pomps* and *Diversions*, at which they could not be present without great *Sin* and *Shame*; without affronting their *Modesty*, and offering a Distast and Horrour to their *Minds*: And *Tertullian* tells us (*z*) that *upon any Man's Conversion to Christianity he immediately abstain'd from the Stage*, and that *his Abstaining was a Principal Sign of his Conversion*. Nay, they were so strict, that (*a*) if any *Pagan*, who was a profess'd *Actor* on, or *Frequenter* on the *Stage*, desir'd to turn *Christian*, he was first to renounce all

(*u*) Dr. Caves Primitive Christianity, Part 2. Chap. 2. Pag 32.

(*x*) Pag 34. Oxon. Edit.

(*y*) Page 106.

(*z*) Lib. de Spectaculis, pag. 700.

(*a*) Concilium Eliberinum, Can. 62. Theodoret. contra Graecos infideles, Lib. 8.

all such *Actings*, and promise to forsake them for the future, before he could be admitted into the *Church* by *Baptism:* And if any *Christian* did afterward (b) *act* upon the *Stage*, he was excluded from the *Church*, the *Sacraments*, and all *Christian Society*, until he had utterly abjur'd the same, and solemnly protested to return to it no more. And the Reason assign'd is, because *it was not fit, that the Modesty and Honour of Christ's Church should be defil'd by such a polluted and infamous Contagion.* And therefore, I think we have greater Reason to imitate the *Jews* and *purest Christians* in this Case, than the *Pagan Greeks* and *Romans*.

(b) Concilium Eliberinum; *Can.* 62. Cypriani *ad* Eucratium *Epist. lib.* 1, *Epist.* 19.

But to urge this farther. In all the *Scriptures* both of the *Old* and *New Testament*, there is not a Word to recommend such Diversions. In all the *Ecclesiastical Writers* of the four first *Centuries*, there is no tone Expression in Favour of the *Stage*, and there are very few who do not set themselves directly against it. The *Fathers* constantly express their Resentments, without any Limitation, and exclaim against it, as a thing positively evil in it self, as the very Nest of *Iniquity*, the Synagogue

of

of *Satan*, the Bane of *Religion*, the *Pomp
and Vanity of this wicked World*,
which a *Christian* renounceth in his
Baptismal Vow, and the In-let to all
Vice and *Profaneness*, and constantly
plead for its total Suppression. I shall
not mention any particular Quotations,
because Mr. *Collier* hath (*c*) largely
given us the Sence of the *Fathers* on
this Subject, and yet he hath not said
half which may be produced. However, it may not be improper to observe, that they all condemn the *Plays*
for two Reasons.

First, because of their *Immorality*
and *Profaneness*. This *Argument* hath
been applyed by several eminent *Pens*
against our *English Stage*; and yet
they will not reform, but continue
as bad as ever, as if they resolved that
nothing should reclaim them.

Secondly, They were condemn'd upon
the Score of *Idolatry*. As they represented some Parts of *Pagan Worship*, so
under that Notion they were unlawful
to *Christians*. Mr. *Collier* indeed tells us
(*d*) that since this *Reason* expir'd in a
great Measure with the *Heathen Religion*,
he should not insist upon it. He was
willing to own them not guilty. However,

(*c*) *His
Short View
of the Stage,
from page
250, to page
275.*

(*d*) *De-
fence of his
Short View,
page 133.*

ever, they have since reviv'd even the
Pagan Superstition; as if they would
give Force to all the *Arguments* of the
Primitive Fathers, and put it out of any
Man's Power, to make an *Apology* for
them. Accordingly (*e*) the *Pictures* of
these *Gods* are represented on the *Stage,*   (*e*) The
their *Temples* are fill'd with *Votaries,*   Faithful Ge-
their *Altars* flame with *Sacrifices,* and   neral, *page*
the *Attributes* of the true *God* are a-   25.
scrib'd to t he *Devil* and *Pagan Deities.*
This is the *Reformation* in the *Play-*
House, and what they aim at is too
plainly seen.

If we do but tell them of a Crime
from which they are free, it is the
ready Way to make them guilty: And
if we do but tell them of a Fault in
the *Heathen Poets,* they will exceed it, as if they resolved to out-vye
with them in every exceptionable Passage, and make the *Play-House* a common
Receptacle for all Uncleanness. Mr.   (*f*) Short
Collier only tells us, that (*f*) *Chærea* in   View of the
Terence falls into an ill Rapture after   Stage, *page*
his Success in *Debauching* a Virgin; and   86.
since, we find this Rapture far out done   (*g*) The
in (*g*) a *Modern Tragedy* upon the like   Rival Bro-
Occasion.   thers, *page*
72.

P 3   It

It is therefore a dreadful thing to consider the Guilt of our *present Stage*, after all the Attempts for a *Reformation*, and Bearing so long in Hopes thereof; and it is as strange to hear others excuse all this, by saying, *That the Poets and Actors design no Harm, it is their Maintainance, what they do is but in Jest, and intended only for Diversion.*

If *Designing no Harm* is an Excuse for the *Stage*, I doubt it may be pleaded for *Common Swearers*, *Cursers*, *Drunkards*, and *Profaners* of the *Lords Day*. All these will as truly say they do mean no *Harm*. This Argument will take off the Guilt from all *Sins* of *Ignorance*, But if *Harm* attends it, no Excuse can be admitted. We must not do Evil, that Good may come of it; and much less can we excuse our Evil by saying, we intend no *Harm*. If it must be allowed, because some are thereby maintain'd, this will be a good Plea for the *Roman Stews*, our *Common Beggars*, all sorts of *Rogues* and *Vagabonds*, and all unlawful Callings whatsoever. This was an Argument (*b*) of *Demetrius* for *Pagan Worship*. it pleaded against suppressing

(*b*) Act 19. 25.

of

of all *Monasteries*, and might have hinder'd our *Reformation* from *Popery*, and we may as well argue, that there are a great many People maintain'd by the *War*, and therefore we must never have Peace. If it is an ill Calling, the greater Number concern'd makes it so much the worse; and the Enemy thereby is become more formidable. If they were to be encouraged in their Proceedings, because they could not live without it, there is no *High-Way-Man*, *Thief*, or *Pickpocket*, who would not urge the same Excuse at the Bar. But if Necessity made them at first think of this way for a Livelihood, the same Necessity may make them again think of some other.

The Excuse that *it is but in Jest* was never admitted among the *Heathen*. *Xenophon* (i) tells us of a *Persian School-master* who excercised his *Scholars* to lye, backbite and cheat, and made them practise these things in jest among themselves. By this *Method* it happened, that his *Scholars*, being apt to learn, began to deceive, cheat and steal from others, and even from their Friends; and tho'. this *Schoolmaster* had taught them, that they ought not to do it, and intended

(i) De Cyri Instituti-one, *lib.* 1.

only

only to expose *Vice*, that they might abhor it; yet what was taught by *Example*, could not be prevented by *Precept*, until the *Persians* made a *Law* to forbid such *Representations*. When (k) *Solon* beheld *Thespis* acting a *Tragedy*, wherein there were many *Lyes* and *Cheats*, he asked; If he was not a-sham'd to lye and cheat before so great a Multitude, in so notorious a Manner? To which *Thespis* answer'd, That there was no Hurt in it; it was all in *Jest*, and nothing in *Earnest*. But *Solon* immediately stroke his Staff upon the Ground with Indignation, and made this Answer; *If we commend or approve of this Play, the Jest will turn to Earnest, and we shall quickly find it in our Bargains.* This was an Answer full to the Purpose, and perhaps for this Reason, he is burlesqu'd in a modern *Comedy*. *Horace* was (l) also of the Opinion, that *Trifles and Jests will bring a Man into real Mischiefs and Inconveniencies.* Besides, *Solomon* tells us (m) that they are *Fools*, who thus *make a mock at Sin*, and (n) *A companion of* such *fools shall be destroy'd:* And that (o) *As a mad man, who casteth firebrands, arrows and death; So*

(k) Plu-tarch *and* Di-ogenes Laer; tius, *de Vitâ Solonis.*

(l) De Ar-te Poëticâ. *——— Hae nugae seria ducent in mala.*

(m) Prov. 14. 9.
(n) Prov. 13. 20.

(o) Prov. 26. 18, 19.

is

is he that deceiveth his neighbour, and faith; Am not I in sport? And St. *Paul* speaking (*p*) of some things, which were not to be *named among Christians*, mentions the three *Stage-Vices*, namely, *Filthiness, Foolish talking* and *Jesting*, wich he again tells us, *are not convenient*. The *Advocates* of the *Stage* excuse what is said, because it is only a *Jesting Matter*. St. *Paul* condemns it for the same Reason; and therefore, if their *Argument* is good, the *Apostle* is mistaken. Besides the *Stage* jests with such things, as are not to be jested with. Can we *swear, curse, blaspheme, mock God, ridicule Religion,* and *burlesque* the *Scriptures* in *Jest?* Can we make a *Jest* of *Hell,* and not expose our selves to the Miseries of that *Place?* These *Sports* and *Jests* call for *Judgments* in earnest. A *Tempest* on the *Stage* may afterward be sent on the *Nation. Magical Representations* may provoke *God,* until the *Devil* is let loose to act more dismal *Tragedies.* When *Devils* carry Men to *Hell* in Jest, and the *Stage* opens for this Purpose, we may dread the Fate of *Korah, Dathan* and *Abiram*; and whilst *Fire* and *Brimstone* is raining in the *Play-House,* we may

(p) Ephes. 5. 3, 4.

tremble

tremble to think on *Sodom* and *Gomorrah*.

In the Midst of these our late Representations, *God* hath bless'd this Nation with wonderful Success, with signal and unexpected Victories, with a Prospect both of *Peace abroad* and *Peace at Home*; but if his *Goodness*, his *Forbearance* and *Long suffering* do not *lead us to repentance*, if we thus suffer him to be despis'd, affronted and abus'd, if he hath Cause to complain, that his *Name continually every day is blasphemed*, his Mercies may yet be turn'd into Judgments, and *a worse thing* may *come upon us* for so great an Ingratitude.

To conclude, When *Religion* and the *Scriptures* are made the Jest of the *Play-House*, when *God* and his *Judgments* are despis'd and slighted, then it is high Time to suppress such Places of *Iniquity*, and they, who value any thing that is sacred, ought to oppose such, who thus profane it. When the *Poet's Hands*, like *Ishmael*, are *against every man*, then *every mans hand* ought to be *against them*. The *Actors* pretend to be *Her Majesties Servants*, and yet value not Her Orders, but provoke

God

God to blaft Her Defigns for the Good of this Nation. Whilft others expound the *Scriptures* for the *Salvation* of Mankind, thefe *ungodly* Men *pervert* them (as it is to be fear'd) *to their own*, and their Hearers *Deftruction*: And if the *Reformation* of Manners, which they pretend to aim at fhould fucceed accordingly, *God* muft be dethron'd, the *Devil* ador'd, *Virtue* fupprefs'd, *Vice* encourag'd, the *Churches* deftroy'd, and then the *Play-Houfes* will be frequented. In fhort, *Hell* is broken loofe among us, and we have *Schools* erected in feveral Cities of this Nation, to teach the *Language of the Damn'd*. The Horrour of their Expreffions needs no farther Difcovery, and calls for a greater Warmth than I am able to exprefs. I therefore beg and intreat all fuch, who have any Regard for the Glory of *God*, any Hopes of his *Mercy*, or Fear of his *Judgments*, any Value for the *Scriptures*, or Love for *Religion*, that they will abftain from fuch Places, and *not be partakers with them in their evil deeds*, and that they will in their feveral Stations, difcourage all fuch *Acts*, as a Scandal to *Chriftianity*, and a Method which may provoke *God*, after

ter so many *Mercies* abus'd, to enter into *Judgment*. We justly abhor the *Popish Mass*, because they pray to *Saints* departed, and can we think it a less Crime, to be present in those Assemblies, where the *Devil* is invok'd, and his Name frequently mention'd in their Ejaculations? If it was the Honour of our *Fore-Fathers*, to oppose the Worshipping of *Saints*, and the *Ave-Marias*, even to Death, their Memory will be a Disgrace to us, if we oppose not those, who like the *Indians* worship the *Devil*, with an *Hail Power: beneath*, as if we thought, that such *Abominations* did not deserve our Resentments. I know not what can excuse our Remisness, unless we imagine, that the *Devils* in *Hell* ought to have that Respect, which we justly deny to the *Virgin Mary*, and the *Saints* in *Heaven*. I beg, that such as read this Book, will frequently put up their Prayers to *God*, to deliver us from such monstrous Practices. The *Psalmist* hath long since (*q*) given us a Pattern. *O God, how long shall the Adversary do this dishonour? How long shall the enemy blaspheme thy name? for ever? Arise, O God, maintain thine own cause: remember how the foolish man*

(q) Psal. 74. 11 and 23.

man blasphemeth thee daily. And I hope, that all good *Christians* will learn to abhor the *Abominations* of the Play-House, as often as they use the Expressions in our Excellent *Litany*.

From all the Deceits of the World, the Flesh and the Devil ; and *From Hardness of Heart, and Contempt of thy Word and Commandment* ;

Good Lord deliver us.

Copies

Copies of several *Prefentments* of
the *Grand Juries*, againſt the
Play-Houſe lately erected in the
City of *Briſtol*.

Tha Preſentment *of the* Grand Jury,
met at the General Quarter-Seſſions
of the Peace, *the Sixth Day of* December, 1704.

VVE the Grand Jurors for our
Sovereign Lady the Queen,
for the Body of the County of this
City do, as in Conſcience and Duty
bound, acknowledge the good Endeavours that have been uſed by this
Worſhipful Bench, for ſome Years paſt,
to diſcourage Immorality and Profaneneſs, by bringing under Reſtraint, and
endeavouring to ſuppreſs thoſe evil
Methods by which they were promoted and encouraged, ſuch as *Muſick-Houſes*, and other *Lewd* and *Diſorderly
Houſes*, the *Exerciſe* of *Unlawful Games*,
the *extravagant Number* of *Ale-Houſes*,
Tipling

Tipling, or *idle Walking* on the *Lord's Day, profane Curfing* and *Swearing, Acting* of *Plays* and *Interludes*; which Endeavours tending to *God's* Glory, your Zeal and Forwardnefs therein hath juftly gain'd you the Efteem and Honour of all good People of this City and the adjacent Counties, to whom you have not only fhewed a good Example, but encouraged to profecute fo good a Work: and we are alfo with all humble Submiffion bound to reprefent the fad Apprehenfions we have of the fame Evils again breaking in upon us worfe than formerly, by the *Increafe* of the *great Number* of *Tipling-Houfes,* kept by fuch, who in Contempt of Juftice fell Ale without Licenfe, (the *Lord's Day* being much profan'd by *Tipling* in fuch *Houfes*) and alfo by the great Concourfe of People in publick Places under Pretence of hearing News on that Day. But that which puts us more efpecially under thefe fad *Apprehenfions,* is the late Permiffion given to the *Publick Stage,* within the Liberties of this City, from whence fome have conceiv'd Hopes, it fhall be tolerated always; and Countenance, or at leaft Connivance giv'n to *Acting* of *Plays* and *Interludes* within this City and County, which (if it should be) will exceedingly eclipse the good Order and Government of this City, corrupt and debauch our *Youth*, and utterly ruin many *Apprentices* and *Servants*, already so *Unruly* and *Licentious*, that they are with great Difficulty kept under any reasonable Order or Government by their Masters.

We could wish that these our sad Apprehensions were groundless: But, when in all Ages, *Acting of Plays* and *Interludes* hath been attended with all manner of *Profaneness*, *Lewdness*, *Murthers*, *Debauching* and *Ruining Youth* of *both Sexes*, infusing *Principles* of *Idleness* and *Extravagancy* into all People that resort to them. We hope your Worships seriously will consider of Effectual Methods to prevent them, and with the greatest Zeal and Fervency will put the same in Execution, when it is apparent that all the Methods to correct and keep them within modest Bounds (where they are tolerated) have proved ineffectual: And all Wise Men are convinced that there is no Methods of hindering or preventing their Mischiefs, but by totally suppressing

preffing them. Your Worfhips Tafk
is not fo difficult, Preventing Reme-
dies being more natural and eafy than
Punifhing. And we humbly conceive
you have Reafons more cogent to ftir
you up to this Work, than offer themfelves to Cities and Places where they
have been tolerated, abounding with
Gentry and *Nobility,* whofe *Eftates* and
Leafure render fuch Extravagancies
more tolerable. But if in fuch Places
their direful and calamitous Effects
have been fo fenfibly felt, how much
more in a City not to be upheld but
by Trade and Induftry, will they be
infupportable? We therefore do not
doubt but all the due Care will be taken by your Worfhips to redrefs and
prevent thefe Grievances, that a Stop
may be put to the further Progrefs of
Immorality and *Profanenefs,* and the
Work of *Reformation* carried on, fo
earneftly prefs'd by Her Majefty's Proclamation, whofe Pious Endeavours
God has fo fignally owned in the great
Victories with which he hath bleffed
Her Arms, whofe Glorious Example
we doubt not but you will follow, to
your lafting Honour and Renown, and

Q

the

the Encouragement and Comfort of all good Citizens.

Walter Chapman, &c.

Part of the Prefentment *of the* Grand Jury, *met at the General* Quarter-Seffions *of the* Peace, *the* 10th *Day of* Auguft, 1706.

WE prefent Mr. *Power*, and his Company, for Acting of *Plays* within the Liberties of this City, without your Worfhips Leave and Confent.

Ifaac Foord, &c.

Part of the Prefentment *of the* Grand Jury, *met at the General* Affize *of* Goal Delivery, *the* 15th *Day of* Auguft, 1706.

WE muft not here omit to Declare how much it afflicts our Thoughts, That after fo great Obligations to *Divine Benignity* in the late wonderful Revolution: And in Her Majefty's fe-
curing

curing to us, our *Religion*, *Liberties*, and *Properties*, then restored : And in Her Pious Zeal to convey these *Privileges* to Posterity by Her repeated *Proclamations* against all *Vice* and *Immorality*, newly rehearsed to us, that yet the worthy Designs thereof are not effectually attained, nor *Wickedness* so intirely suppressed by the active Endeavours of our Magistrates, as we could heartily wish. For which End, we would humbly recommend to Your Worships utmost Care and unanimous Zeal, to search out and pursue the most effectual and lawful Methods for crushing the newly erected *Play-House*, that *School of Debauchery* and *Nursery of Profaneness*, where *Vice* and *Lewdness* appear Bare-faced, and Impudent, *Swearing* notoriouslyPractised and Recommended : The Danger and Growth of which, we have been seasonably warned against by our Right Reverend the Lord *Bishop*, and other Reverend *Divines* from the *Pulpit*.

Richard Leversedge, &c.

Appendix

Cancel leaf B1^r from the Lowe
copy at Harvard (Thr. 417.06*)

HELL upon *EARTH:*

OR, THE

LANGUAGE

OF THE

𝔓𝔩𝔞𝔶-𝔥𝔬𝔲𝔰𝔢.

CHAP I.

The Obstinacy of the Stage.

THE *English Stage* taking a Liberty unknown in any *Heathen*, and notoriously *Scandalous* in a *Christian* Country, Mr. *Jeremy Collier* first began the *Attack* against them, in his Book, intituled, *A Short View of the English Stage ;* wherein he fully convicted their *Poets* of *Immodesty* and *Pro-*

B *faneness,*